GW01018166

JACK CASEY
The Sunderland Assassin

Archie Potts

Bewick Press

© 1991 Archie Potts

First published in Great Britain by
Bewick Press,
132 Claremont Road,
Whitley Bay,
Tyne and Wear,
NE 26 3TX

ISBN 0 - 9516056 -2-3

All rights are reserved. No part of this publication may be reproduced, transmitted or stored in any retrieval system, in any form or by any means, without permission in writing from the publisher.

Printed and bound in Great Britain
by Mayfair Print Group, William Street, Sunderland.

ACKNOWLEDGEMENTS

I am grateful to Mr John Casey for allowing me access to family records, and to the staffs of the British Newspaper Library at Colindale, Newcastle Central Library, and the Sunderland Central Library for enabling me to consult their files of newspapers and periodicals. Photographs have been obtained from several sources and I am grateful, again, to John Casey; and also to Neil Sinclair and the Sunderland staff of the Tyne and Wear Museum Service for providing photographs of 'old Sunderland'; to Mr John Brown, manager of the Hendon Gardens Hotel in Sunderland, for letting me use photographs from his boxing collection; and to the editors of the Newcastle Chronicle and Journal, and the Sunderland Echo, for giving me permission to use press photographs. I should like to thank Vic Hardwicke and John Upton for their assistance in compiling Jack Casey's fight record; and to members of the Sunderland Ex-Boxers Association and the Tyneside Ex-Boxers Association and others who knew Jack Casey or saw him box. I should like to thank Leigh Clarke for preparing the manuscript. The final outcome, however, is my responsibility and any errors and omissions should be laid at my door.

Archie Potts

Table of contents:

INTRODUCTION

In the 1920's and '30's, North East England was one of the main centres for boxing in the United Kingdom. Major promotions were held on a regular basis in Newcastle, Sunderland, West Hartlepool and Middlesbrough, and minor bouts were staged at dozens of small halls throughout the region. The crowds turned out in force to watch their local favourites in action. During the 1920's, both St James' Hall, in Newcastle, and the Holmeside Stadium, in Sunderland, had seating for 3,000 spectators and big fight nights were usually a sell-out. These promotions were underpinned by a network of gymnasiums where boxers went to train and develop their skills. It has been said that the best fighter is a hungry fighter, and there was no lack of young men in the depressed North East prepared to lace on the gloves and try their luck in the ring. It was a promoters' market and boxers usually accepted, without demur, the rates of pay they were offered. Money, however, was not the sole attraction. Many boxers loved the sport with its challenge and excitement, and for some it brought a measure of fame.

The North East of this period produced a host of good fighters, too numerous to mention here, but any list would have to include: Tyneside's Billy Charlton, Mickey Mcguire, Benny Sharkey, Jim Shippen and Tommy Watson; Wearside's Douglas Parker, Charlie McDonald, Roy Mills and the brothers, Billy and Tom Smith; West Hartlepool's Jack London, Jackie Horseman and Teddy Gardner; and Middlesbrough's Harry Craster. Most of these boxers were capable of fighting for a British championship, and some of them became champions. But perhaps the best remembered name - certainly on Wearside - is that of Jack Casey, whose boxing career spanned the years from 1926 to 1942. He started as a flyweight and boxed his way up the divisions to heavyweight. He fought some of the best boxers of his time and was never knocked out in his entire career.

Jack Casey had a unique style of fighting, moving forward in a crouch with his jaw exposed and taking any number of blows on the chin, in order to land one of his own. He would wear an opponent down with relentless pressure and then move in with a two-handed assault, or, as Peter Wilson, the boxing writer, graphically put it:

> *"Casey's distinctly original method of waging war was more or less to tuck the thumbs into his navel and come in flat-footed with his chin stuck out, challengingly. In the early stages of all his fights you could see his opponents thinking with sceptical delight that such a thing - and such a target - could not be true. As far as the second part was concerned, they were right. Casey's chin was too tough to be true. Time after time, strong men would wear themselves out, smashing away at this block of granite, until , arm-weary, they became an easy prey for Casey, in the later rounds."*

Casey was working as a newspaper-boy when he fought his first professional fight and was sometimes billed as Newsboy Casey, but, as he gained a reputation for toughness and durability, he became known as 'Cast iron' Casey, and it was Jim Smith , the Lancashire promoter, who, after witnessing Casey's demolition tactics in the ring, dubbed him the 'Sunderland Assassin'.

Casey was a colourful performer and he had that little extra something in his personality which, in the theatre is known as 'star quality' and, in politics, is referred to as 'charisma'. The crowds loved to see him in action and he always gave them value for their money. He became something of a folk hero in his home town of Sunderland, especially to the people of the East End where he lived, and long after his boxing career ended he was one of the best known figures in the town.

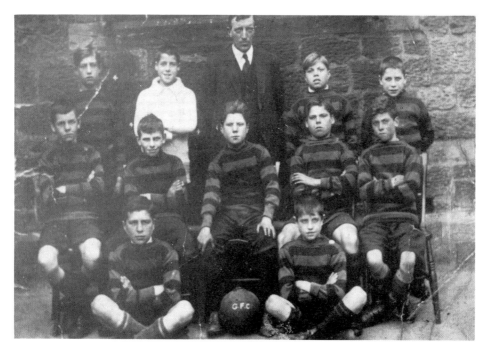

Gray School football team 1922
Jack Casey (captain) with the ball between his feet.

Chapter 1

OPENING ROUNDS

Jack Casey was born on 22 September 1908, in Edward Burdis Street, in the Southwick district of Sunderland, the son of John and Elizabeth Casey, and, at the time of his birth, his father was registered as an apprentice ship rivetter. The Caseys, however, were an East End family and they moved back to Sunderland's old dockside area, shortly after Jack's birth. Jack was brought up in the old tenement buildings of the East End and was educated at the Gray School, a Church of England school founded by a former rector of the parish. Jack's school record suggests that he was an average pupil in most respects. However, he was keenly interested in sport and played centre-forward in the school football team. The school's sports master, J.W.D.Fowler, considered Casey a good soccer prospect, and Mr Fowler certainly knew his subject for he was a Football League referee and once refereed an F.A. Cup Final. Casey was modest about his footballing abilities: "I was just a big bustler." he later recalled. He was also a very good swimmer, an activity he enjoyed throughout his life. When Casey left school, in January 1923, at the age of fourteen, Mr H.Carr, Head Teacher at the Gray School, wrote in his school leaving report:

> ' He is a boy of good disposition, very willing and very
> regular in his attendance at school. He is very good at sports
> having been captain of the school football team for the past
> year. He is honest, straightforward and reliable. '

After Jack left school, he worked as a newspaper boy, selling newspapers from a pitch on the corner of Burleigh Street and High Street East. His entry into the ranks of professional boxing was by chance. The young Casey was a regular attender at the boxing matches held at the Holmeside Stadium, and he was there on 17 July 1926 when one of the contestants in a novices' flyweight competition withdrew. Jack Casey, then a seventeen year old newspaper seller, was drafted in as a last minute replacement. That night, Casey knocked out W.Teasdale, in the first round of his heat, and, in the final, he boxed a four-round draw with Jim Britton. The prize money of fifteen shillings was shared between the two finalists. The boxing correspondent of the *Sunderland Echo* observed: 'They were a very clever pair of boxers to be in the novice class'; and Alfred Black, one of the Black Brothers who owned the Stadium, wrote in his diary: 'Casey looks good.'

After this successful introduction to the fight game, Casey joined Duggie Morton's school of boxing. Every Tuesday and Thursday evening, after he had sold his newspapers, he attended Morton's gym, and on other evenings he put in some roadwork, usually jogging up and down the High Street bank. Casey's father had done some boxing, as a young man, and he was a strong influence on his son's career. John Casey was always ready with advice and encouragement, and he was usually in Jack's corner at fights.

On 6 November 1926, Jack Casey entered another novices' competition at the Stadium, where he fought a return fight with Jim Britton, in the first heat. This time, Britton won a narrow points victory over six rounds; and went on to be stopped in the first round by E. Place in the final of the competition. Although Casey had lost his heat, Duggie Morton considered him to be ready to move out of the novices' class, and, on 20 December, he was matched with George Willis, a hard-hitting Tyne Dock fighter at North Shields. The result was a draw, after a hard-fought battle between two fighters who scorned defence. The contest was watched by the coloured boxing promoter, Joe Johns, who was so impressed that he matched the two for a return contest, at his hall in Jarrow. This time, Casey scored a decisive points win over six rounds and was firmly launched on a boxing career.

Jack Casey fought thirty times in 1927, scoring twenty-two wins, six losses and two draws. It was a promising start to a career in the ring. He fought mainly in halls in the Tyne and Wear area, and against local opponents. After points victories over George Willis and Young Scott, he lost a points decision to Teddy Walsh at Stoker Allen's South Shields hall and another to Alf Bainbridge, at North Shields. Casey then drew with Eddie McGurk, under Phil Dooley's promotion, at the Tyne Dock Coliseum. This was a non-stop action contest and the crowd clamoured for a return match, which they got a week later. This time, McGurk, the son of former boxer Pat McGurk, and rated a good prospect, won narrowly on points over six rounds. Casey then chalked up five consecutive wins, against Alf Smith, Joe Kennedy, Eddie McGurk (in a rubber match), Teddy Walsh and Owen McIvor. Casey next met up again with Jim Britton, the youth who had beaten him in the novices' competition the previous year. At this meeting, Britton scored another narrow points victory over Casey, and when they were re-matched, a week later, the result was a draw. Casey went on to score eleven consecutive wins, over Barney Ward, Slogger Bingham, Jack Graham, Phil Guerin, Owen McIvor, Tommy East, Danny Veitch, Young Josephs, Joe Woodie, Joe Kennedy and Pat Crawford.

On 4 November 1927, Casey faced Peel Bell, at the Infantry Drill Hall, Carlisle. In the eighth round, Bell landed a hard right on Casey's ear which caused severe swelling. Casey wanted to box on, but the referee was concerned that his ear should suffer no further damage and he persuaded Casey to retire. Thus Bell was the first man to stop Casey inside the distance. A cauliflower ear did not stop Casey for long, however, and, within a week, he was slugging it out over ten rounds with Bob Phillips at Sunderland. He fought Phillips in a re-match, three weeks later; then lost to Pat Crawford with more ear trouble, in the fourth round; and followed up with a points win over Dave O'Dowd. Casey ended the year by travelling to Leeds, where he was beaten on points by the Barnsley lightweight, Jim Birch, who proved too experienced for the Sunderland youngster.

Casey was proving himself a crowd-pleaser: he was tough and aggressive in the ring and the fans loved his style. He had no problem in picking up fights. In 1928, he had twenty-eight fights with twenty-two wins, three losses and three draws, maintaining the good start he had made the previous year.

He began the year by stopping local rival, Con Tansey, in seven rounds (cut lip) and Young Griffo in seven (busted lip), then beat Pat Crawford on a disqualification in the fifth round. Casey's next opponent was Tommy Woods, a member of the famous fighting family from Bonnybridge, and they boxed a draw at Tyne Dock. Casey then travelled to Leeds, for his second fight in that city, where he beat Billy Mack of Huddersfield on points over ten rounds.

Casey's first defeat of the year was at the hands of Jack Turner. Turner was a member of Len Johnson's boxing booth team. He was very tall for a lightweight, with a long reach, and he successfully tied up the young tearaway to win on points over ten rounds. Casey then scored points victories over Andy Keating and Joe Grewer.

*Corner of Burleigh St and High St East
where Jack Casey sold newspapers.*

Chapter 2

MOVING UP THE BILL

Casey left Sunderland, in June 1928 after a tiff with his fiancee, Elizabeth Lincoln. Miss Lincoln, apparently, wanted Casey to wear a collar and tie, when they went out together, but Jack refused and, after a row, he boarded an excursion train to Manchester. He stayed at his uncle's home, in Ashton-under-Lyne, and picked up a couple of fights in local rings. He beat Terry Donlan in seven rounds and Stan Bradbury on points over ten rounds. Harry 'Kid' Furness, who was then promoting at the Adelphi Athletic Club in Salford, matched Casey with local lad, Al Kenny, over fifteen rounds. This was the first time Casey had fought over this distance and the first time he had enjoyed star billing, for which he was paid £3. Furthermore, the referee was the former British heavyweight champion, Bombadier Wells. When, at the end of the fight, Wells announced his decision to be a draw, he was met by a storm of booing from the crowd who believed that Casey had done enough to win. The booing of the normally popular Billy Wells made headlines in the next day's newspapers, and this was the first time Jack Casey got his name in the national press.

Casey continued his spell of fighting in Lancashire rings. He fought his second fifteen-rounder against Charlie Dickenson, at Openshaw, losing on points; knocked out Jim Harrison in three rounds, at Ashton; beat Jock McFarlane on points, over fifteen rounds at Royton; and lost on points over fifteen rounds to Jack Hines, at Manchester.

Sometime in late August, Jack's father rang to say that he had arranged a return match for him with Charlie Dickenson at the Sunderland Stadium, and so Casey returned to his home town. He beat Joe Grewer, the original 'cast-iron man', in seven rounds, three weeks before disposing of Charlie Dickenson over the same distance. He returned to Sunderland wearing a collar and tie, making possible a reconciliation with Lizzie Lincoln, and they were married the following year.

Casey lost his third contest of the year against Young Griffo at St James' Hall, Newcastle. Griffo fought on the retreat and counter-boxed his way to a fifteen round points victory over Casey. Casey then won eight consecutive fights, over Paul Maguire, Lion Smith, Ernest Kay (twice), Ted Abbott, Peter Bottomley, Charlie Lee, Alec Law and Dino Guselli. His final fight of the year was a third meeting with Ernest Kay, at West Hartlepool, which was declared a draw.

Casey described Dino Guselli, a former Olympic champion, as the toughest opponent he had met to date, and it was during his fight with the hard-hitting Italian that Casey claimed he first realised the full strength of his jaw. Guselli hit him with everything he had, but Casey did not go down. After the fight, Joe Tolley, the Royton promoter, said: 'Where did you get that cast-iron jaw, Casey?' and, according to Casey, the label stuck. Joe Grewer had been known as the 'cast-iron man' until Casey had disposed of him, two months before, therefore the title was, so to speak, vacant. Casey never lost it.

Casey was now boxing as a welterweight, in twelve and fifteen rounders. In 1929, he had thirty fights with thirteen wins, thirteen losses and four draws. His boxing record for 1929, therefore, appears less impressive than his previous two years, but he was now fighting top of the bill or chief supporting bout fighters and finding the going harder. British boxing during this period had great depth, there were many fighters with a wide variety of styles: classical boxers and sluggers, experienced fighters on the way down and younger fighters on the way up. The crowds knew their boxing and wanted to see evenly-matched men, not one-sided contests, and the promoters did their best to oblige. This meant that there were few easy fights, and when fighting every fortnight, as did Casey, it was impossible for a boxer to be on top form in every fight and any weaknesses were likely to be ruthlessly exposed by an opponent in the ring.

In 1929, Casey lost four times to Albert Johnson (brother of the more famous Len), a coloured fighter from Manchester. The first contest took place at the Sunderland Stadium, on 1 June 1929. Johnson was taller than Casey and he hit Casey's face at will, cutting both of Casey's eyes and prompting Casey's corner to throw in the towel at the end of the seventh round. They met again, over twelve rounds, at Leeds, a fortnight later. Again Johnson peppered Casey with his left hand in the opening rounds and, although Casey made some good two-handed rallies, Johnson got on top as the fight progressed and won on points. Johnson won again on points, over fifteen rounds, when they met at Middlesbrough on 1 August; and they met a fourth time, on 19 October, when Johnson opened up some cuts on Casey's face, forcing the referee to stop the fight in the sixth round. Johnson had the measure of Casey: he was the only man to defeat Casey four times and to stop him twice within the distance, although Casey was perhaps unfortunate to meet Albert Johnson when the Manchester fighter was at his peak, for in August 1929, Johnson fought Jim Shippen of Jarrow for the Northern Area welterweight title.

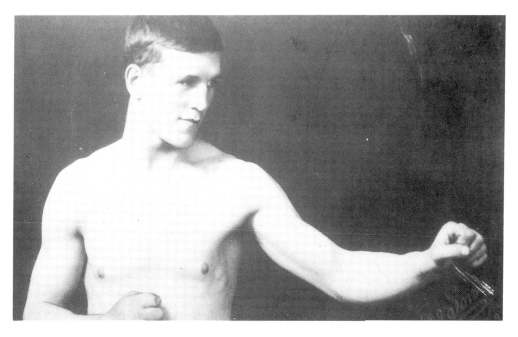

JACK HARBIN
The Usworth miner who twice defeated Casey in 1929

7

Casey was beaten twice on points by Jack Harbin. Harbin was a miner from Usworth and his uncle, also named Jack, had been a well-known bare knuckle fighter. Harbin was an exponent of the traditional English style of boxing, with the emphasis on the straight-left, in complete contrast to Casey's crouching style and two-handed attacks. They first met at Sunderland Stadium on 12 January 1929, as the main supporting bout over twelve rounds to the Sonny Bird-Franz Kruppel top of the bill. It proved a hard and entertaining fight, with Jack Harbin keeping Casey at bay with a left jab, and winning the decision on points. They met again at St James' Hall, on 2 March, in another twelve round contest, which one boxing reporter described as 'a cracker all the way'. Casey did most of the attacking, but Harbin's straight left held him off, and, in the third round, a right hook closed Casey's left eye. Not that this worried Casey who continued to tear into Harbin and, in the sixth round, he caught the pitman with a right to the jaw. This shook Harbin, but he boxed his way out of trouble and piled up sufficient points in the later rounds to win the bout. Jack Harbin's boxing career spanned the years 1925-31 and he moved to Leeds, shortly after his fights with Casey, where he became very popular with the Yorkshire boxing fans.

Casey lost two contests on points to the Newcastle fighter, George Willis, one of the North's top welterweights. Willis had won a boxing competition at the age of ten and he turned professional in 1924, at the age of fifteen. His ring experience included working in Gage's boxing booth at Ashington. Willis was a tough fighter, with a piston-rod left hand which he used to good effect in his contests with Casey.

Casey also lost a fifteen rounds points decision to the blond German welterweight, Franz Kruppel, who spent some time in Sunderland, in order to gain experience in British rings. Casey pressed for a return contest which he won on points and many considered this victory over the highly-rated German fighter to be Casey's best performance up to that time.

Another defeat for the 'cast-iron' man was at the hands of Pat O'Brien, at the Leeds National Sporting Club. Casey recalled that when he accepted the fight, he had never heard of O'Brien, and no-one seemed to know anything about the 'mystery man'. In the ring, O'Brien showed himself to be anything but a novice and he boxed cleverly to beat Casey on points over fifteen rounds. After the fight, O'Brien revealed to Casey that he had previously fought under the name Air Mechanic Mills, and Casey then realised that Mills had been a topliner in his day, having gone fifteen rounds with Vince Dundee, at the Royal Albert Hall. Mills was engaged in a comeback under a new name. Casey sought a return match with O'Brien but the air mechanic was unable to arrange leave from the R.A.F. and the fight never took place.

In the same year, Casey also lost on points to the Accrington hard man, Joe Woodruff, and to Glasgow's Willie Upton. Casey fought Fred Oldfield from Doncaster four times in 1929. Casey won a points decision at Leeds; Oldfield reversed the decison at Sunderland; they drew when they met at Hartlepool; and Oldfield won on points in a second meeting at Hartlepool, on 30 December 1929, in what was Casey's last fight of the year.

In 1929, Casey drew with Ted Abbott (twice), Ted Robinson, and notched up victories over Peter Kelly, Tom Gregson, Bob Cockburn, Ted Abbott (in a return), Jack Marshall, Seaman Smart, Alec Thake, Ted Robinson (in a return), Mick Harris and Jim Pearson.

When Jack Harbin was reminded, at a later date, of his victories over Casey, he replied: 'It's a piece of luck I did not have to meet Casey when he was fighting at his best', and, without detracting in any way from modest Jack Harbin's fine performances against Casey, what he said was true. If Albert Johnson or Jack Harbin had met up with Casey, eighteen months later, the results of their contests would most likely have been different. When Casey did meet George Willis for a third time, in March 1931, he reversed the previous verdicts, in a convincing fashion. In 1929, Casey was capable of giving any welterweight in the country a hard fight, but he was yet to reach his peak as a fighter. He liked nothing better than to slug it out toe to toe with an opponent, when his toughness and hard punching would probably bring him victory; and he could overwhelm any boxer without the skill or strength to hold him off. But, he was less successful against accomplished boxers such as Harbin, Johnson and Willis. He was still learning how to break down a tight defence, and he learned the hard way, by taking punishment and suffering defeats. However, his popularity with the fans was never in question. Whatever the result, Casey could be relied upon to put up a good fight.

FRANZ KRUPPEL
the German welterweight

GEORGE WILLIS
from Newcastle upon Tyne

9

Chapter 3

MEETING THE MIDDLEWEIGHTS

During the course of 1930, Jack Casey moved up into the middleweight class, and over the year he marked up twenty five wins against nine losses with one drawn bout. He lost decisions to Archie Sexton, Sandy McKenzie, Charlie McDonald, Joe Lowther and Harry Mason, but it was no disgrace to lose to men of this calibre who were good class fighters.

Jack Casey met Joe Lowther five times in 1930. Lowther was a tough character from Leeds who became Northern Regional middleweight champion in April 1930, and his fights with Casey were ding dong affairs which tempted promoters to match the two again and again in order to determine who was the better man. The fans certainly had no complaints for they saw some good scraps. Casey started the year by losing a fifteen round bout on points to Joe Lowther at Hull. They were re-matched, a fortnight later, by popular demand, when Lowther won again on points. They met, yet again, on 17 August, over twelve rounds at Leeds when Casey won on points; and, at a further meeting on 10 October at Preston, Casey was forced to retire in the eleventh round with a badly cut face. In Casey's last fight of the year on 21 December, he beat Lowther on points over twelve rounds, at Leeds. The score at the year's end, therefore, was Lowther three wins and Casey two.

Casey met Archie Sexton, at the Sunderland Stadium, on 29 March 1930, in what was to be the first of five ring encounters between the two men. The boxing correspondent of the *Sunderland Echo* described the bout as Jack Casey's biggest test to date and this was a fair assessment. Sexton fought 133 contests in his ring career and lost only sixteen times. He figured in eliminators for the British welterweight title and fought for the British middleweight title. Some boxing commentators considered him to be one of the best fighters never to win a title. Fred Charlton, the boxing referee and promoter and a shrewd judge of the fight game, believed that Sexton's failure to win a championship, at either the welter or middleweight level, lay in his weight. Charlton described him as an 'in-between'. Sexton's best fighting weight was 11 stone, but he had to choose between fighting as a trained down welterweight (10 stone 7lb) or as a light middleweight (11 stone 6lb).

Casey was not disgraced in his first fight with Sexton and one local reporter described his performance as 'creditable', although he was outboxed over fifteen rounds by the classy Sexton. There was an ugly incident at the end of the fourth round, when Sexton hit Casey after the bell had sounded. Some sections of the crowd were incensed by his action and the referee had to appeal for calm. However, Sexton's superb boxing skills won over most of the Sunderland fans, who applauded him when he was awarded the verdict. After the

ARCHIE SEXTON
classy boxer
from Bethnal Green

fight, Sexton explained that due to the noise of the crowd, he had not heard the bell.

Casey met Sandy McKenzie, the 'Glasgow Flash', over fifteen rounds at Hartlepool, on 23 April 1930, when the Scottish fighter won on points. They met, in a re-match, a fortnight later, as the main supporting bout in a special bill to mark the opening of New St James' Hall, in Newcastle. The old St James' Hall had been built in 1909 and, in its day, was one of the best boxing stadiums in the country, with a seating capacity of 3,000. But, by the late 1920's, it was looking old and shabby, and it was closed in June 1929 and a completely new building erected on the site with the capacity increased to 5,000. The re-opening took place on 12 May 1930. The top of the bill was a heavyweight contest between Frank Fowler of York and the French heavyweight champion, Maurice Grizell. Sandy McKenzie, described by one local reporter as 'slippery as an eel', again beat Casey on points, over fifteen rounds in 'a rousing contest from start to finish'. McKenzie beat Casey on points over fifteen rounds, at Manchester, later in the year (on 17 November), but, three weeks afterwards, at the same venue, Casey stopped McKenzie, suffering from a cut eye, in the seventh round. When the pair met, on 2 April 1932, eighteen months later, the vastly improved Casey knocked out the Scottish middleweight in the second round of the contest.

In the same month that New St James' Hall was opened, the Black family announced the closure of Sunderland's Holmeside Stadium to make way for the building of a cinema and dance hall on the site. The last boxing bill at the Stadium was on 31 May 1930 and it comprised all local fighters. The two main bouts were : Billy Smith v Douglas Parker, and Jack Casey v Charlie McDonald. Matchmaker, Fred Charlton, was determined to make the last night one to remember, for the four top of the bill fighters had established themselves as the most popular local performers at the Stadium.

The Holmeside Stadium had opened on 29 May 1920, on the site of the former Olympia skating rink. It was a purpose-built boxing stadium, constructed in the shape of a bowl, with a 3,000 seating capacity. Admission prices ranged from 6d to 2s-4d, and many unemployed men spent what little pocket money they had on a weekly visit to the Stadium. Six-round fighters were paid £1 a fight and boxers fighting in the ten to fifteen

CHARLIE McDONALD
popular Sunderland middleweight

rounders received £7-10s, although 'big names' could expect to be paid at higher rates. Casey was paid £12 for his fight with Archie Sexton at the Stadium, in March 1930, and he received £20 for taking on Charlie McDonald. Fred Charlton recalled that there were over 2,000 registered boxers on Wearside, in the 1920's, and there was never any haggling over rates of pay: it was a promoters' market and the average boxer was grateful for a place on the bill. In Fred Charlton's words: ' Most of them knew their trade in greater or lesser degree and all of them knew that, once inside the ropes, they had to fight like blazes, otherwise it would be a long hungry time before they got another scrap'. Indeed, to appear at the Stadium was the ambition of most of Wearside's boxers, for it conferred status as well as putting money in their pockets.

In an attempt to 'raise the tone' of the Stadium, boxers and their seconds were required to wear a collar and tie before they were allowed to enter the premises, and there were cases of collarless boxers sporting white silk mufflers being denied access to the Stadium and having to borrow the appropriate neckwear before they were allowed to proceed to the dressing rooms.

Charlton claimed that the promoters never made a lot of money out of boxing and, if he is correct, then one can only observe that their overhead costs must have been high because their wage costs were very low. Certainly, the decision to close the Stadium made good commercial sense to the site owners, for the *Regal* cinema and *Rink* dancehall which replaced it enjoyed thirty-five years of excellent business. However, it deprived Sunderland of a large boxing stadium and left Newcastle's New St James' Hall the undisputed venue for major boxing matches in North East England. Boxing in Sunderland continued to be carried on at the *Theatre Royal*, where a ring was set up on the stage; and in the Monkwearmouth Miners' Hall in Roker Avenue, and the Pottery Buildings in the town's East End.

The match between Casey and McDonald had only been made possible by Casey's recent move up into the middleweight class, where McDonald had long been established. Both men had started their boxing careers in the same year, although Charlie had come from a boxing family. He was born in Sunderland in 1904, the son of William McDonald, from St Vincent in the West Indies. Billy McDonald had settled in Sunderland and married a local woman, and Charlie was their third son. Billy had been a professional boxer and he kept a gym in the Hendon district of the town which was used by local sportsmen. Charlie, from an early age, wanted to follow his father into the fight game, and he entered the professional ranks in 1925, where he soon established himself in the fifteen rounders. He was a skilful boxer and carried a knockout punch. Indeed, his hard hitting was once held responsible for the death of an opponent. On 12 November 1927, McDonald met Dick Roughly of Barnsley at the Leeds National Sporting Club. The contest was billed for fifteen rounds but was stopped by the referee in the final round and the decision awarded to McDonald. Roughly was rushed to hospital where he died that night. Charlie McDonald was very upset and vowed: 'I'm boxing no more', and, even after he had been persuaded that Roughly's death was not his fault, it was some time before he could bring himself to unleash his powerful right hand.

McDonald's career spanned the years 1925-36, in which he had 165 fights: 111 wins, 43 losses and 11 draws. Fred Charlton believed that, as a boxer, McDonald lacked only one thing: ambition. He prepared carefully for each individual fight, but never planned his career. Charlie took each fight as it came along. However, owing to the colour bar which was then in force in British boxing, he could never have fought for a British title (even though he was born in Sunderland) although he would have been eligible to compete for a British Empire championship in the 1930's, after Larry Gains had broken the colour bar on the holding of British Empire titles in 1931. In the event, he never came into consideration for the highest honours in the game. He had his best chance only a fortnight after his fight with Casey, when he was matched with Len Harvey, at that time British and Empire middleweight champion. A victory or even a good performance against Harvey could have put him in line for a crack at the British Empire middleweight championship. But Charlie McDonald, as he later acknowledged, did one of the silliest things in his life. He decided to travel down to London on his motorcycle with his second riding pillion. Not surprisingly, he was not at his best the next day, when he needed to be. The contest took place at Premierland, on a sweltering hot day, and the attendance was poor. Harvey was on a percentage of the gate and in a foul mood. He decided to make it a short fight and cut loose against McDonald, knocking him out with a body punch, in the second round. McDonald fought for another six years, topping the bill at provincial stadiums and going the distance with such men as Jack Hood, Jack London, and Jock McAvoy, without making the breakthrough into the big time. He retired from the ring in June 1936, in good fighting trim, after a winning streak in which he won eight and drew two of his last ten fights. McDonald was immensely popular in Sunderland, both as a boxer and a man, for he was extremely modest and had great natural dignity.

The clash between the two Sunderland favourites was eagerly anticipated by Wearside's boxing fans. But, when the fight took place, it proved to be something of an anti-climax. Indeed, the opening rounds were so dull that, in the third round, the referee called for more action. Both men knew each other too well. They were both managed by Duggie Morton, who had been reluctant to see them matched, and had seen too much of each other in the gym. McDonald knew better than to slug it out with Casey, so he kept a somewhat subdued Casey at a distance with his left hand, threw in some body punches when he could, and boxed his way to a comfortable points win.

FRED SHAW
Yorkshire middleweight
from Shipley

Casey also lost on points to Harry Mason, the former British lightweight champion, over twelve rounds at Leeds, on 9 November 1930. Mason was known as the 'Little Fiddler' because he played the violin outside the ring, and knew all the fiddles inside it. He proved far too clever for Casey.

In 1930, Casey beat Jerry Daley (twice), Dick Burt, Hal O'Neill (three times), Wattie Wilde, George Porter, Farmer Jackson, Joe Woodruff (three times), Bert Mottram, Pat Casey, Roy Martin, Fred Oldfield, Gunner Ainsley, Ted Coveney, Billy Roberts, and Fred Shaw. Casey drew with the Birmingham middleweight, Jack Haynes, at their first meeting at Barnsley. They were re-matched, at Sunderland, a month later, when Haynes was disqualified in the sixth round for holding.

Casey's most impressive win, in 1930, was his fifteen rounds points victory over Sonny

Bird at Sunderland on 22 February. This was the first time Casey had topped the bill at the Holmeside Stadium and it was his last fight as a welterweight. Bird was a cagey fighter from Chelsea, who had impressed North Eastern fans with his smart boxing skills. He was well aware of Casey's crouching, aggressive style and, for the first two rounds, he adopted ultra defensive tactics. The crowd grew restless at the lack of action and there were shouts of : 'When does the fight start?' 'Stand up and box' and 'Make a fight of it'. Coming out for the third round, Bird responded to the calls by opening up on Casey in his normal style, and the two men went on to give the fans thirteen rounds of high quality boxing. Yet, in spite of his undoubted skill and guile, Bird was unable to master Casey who was awarded the decision on points.

THE STADIUM,
(S U N D E R L A N D).
NEXT SATURDAY.——Commence 7.30.
15 2's International Welter-weight Contest:—
FRANZ KRUPPEL,
(Germany) v.
SONNY BIRD
(London).
Ten Rounds:—L.A.C. DAVIS (Royal Air Force) v. Peter Miller (Sunderland).
Six Rounds:—Charlie Lines (South Shields) v. Jack Curtis (Hartlepool).
Six Rounds:—Alec McBeth (Hetton) v. Harry Buxton (Sunderland).
12 2's Attractive Welter Weight Contest:—
JACK HARBIN v. JACK CASEY
(Usworth)   (Sunderland).
PRICES:—6d 1/-, 1/6, and 2/4.

THE STADIUM.
(SUNDERLAND.)
SATURDAY MARCH 23rd.
15-Rounds Challenge Contest :–
JACK CASEY
(Sunderland) v.
FRANZ KRUPPEL
(Germany).
Ten Rounds " Needle " Contest:—Young Dibbs (Penshaw) v. Young Jacks (Shiney Row).
Six Rounds Contest:—Frank Osborne (Consett) v. Ginger Bell (Newcastle).
Six Rounds Contest:—Bill Slosh (Newcastle) v. Bobby Mason (Sunderland).
12-Rounds Fly-weight Contest—
JACK OVEY v. TOMMY JAMES
(Oldham)   (Gateshead).
PRICES:—6d, 1/-, 1/6, and 2/4.

THE STADIUM
SATURDAY, FEBRUARY 22nd.
15-Rounds Contest:—
JACK CASEY
(Sunderland) v.
SONNY BIRD
(London).
TOMMY MASON v. KELLY SHANKS.
KID ENWRIGHT v. DAN TOKELL.
Other Bouts.
POPULAR PRICES: 6d, 1/6, and 2/4.
FEB. 26:—NOVICES' NIGHT. Entries Wanted.

THE STADIUM.
SATURDAY MARCH 29th.
15-Rounds Contest at 11st.:—
JACK CASEY
(Sunderland) v.
ARCHIE SEXTON
(London)
TOM COWLEY v. JIMMY ROSS.
JOE COWLEY v. BOY MILLS.
Two Six-Rounders and Novice Bouts.
PRICES:—1/-, 2/-, and 3/6.

THE STADIUM
SATURDAY, MAY 31st.
DOUGLAS PARKER
v.
BILLY SMITH
CHARLIE McDONALD
v.
JACK CASEY
OTHER CONTESTS.
PRICES:—1/3, 2/4, and 4/9.

MacDONALD ducks to avoid a right swing from Casey, and (right) a spell of in-fighting. It was the closing night at the Stadium.

—" Sunderland Echo" photograph.

MacDONALD covers up as Casey prepares to attack.

—" Sunderland Echo" photograph.

The last night at the Stadium.
*Cartoon from **Sunderland Echo** 1 June 1930*

Chapter 4

INTO THE BIG TIME

In 1931, Casey made the breakthrough into big time boxing. He started with a win over Joe Woodruff, on New Year's Day, and then beat Archie Sexton, on 3 January, the Londoner having to retire in the ninth round with a cut eye. A fortnight later, Casey lost a twelve rounds points decision to Fred Shaw, at Leeds. Shaw came from Shipley and was Yorkshire's pride. He was a good stylist and could take a punch. The two men were matched against each other six times in their boxing careers. Nine days later, Casey was in action against the British welterweight champion, Jack Hood, who coolly and methodically boxed his way to a points win over his heavier opponent. Casey then lost on points over ten rounds to the Bath middleweight, Phil Green, and lost a return match against Fred Shaw on points, over twelve rounds, at Leeds. But, out of Casey's next fifteen fights, he won thirteen and drew two. He won ten of these fights inside the distance and it was at this time that Jack Smith, the Lancaster promoter, dubbed him the 'Sunderland Assassin'. He forced the retirement of Shaw (at their fourth meeting), Sonny Doke, Glen Moody, George Willis and Jack O'Brien; and knocked out Jack O'Brien (in a return match), Jack Haynes (twice), George Gordon and Dick Bartlett.

JACK HOOD
British Welterweight Champion

Casey's fight with George Willis took place at New St James' Hall, on 9 March. They had met twice before, in 1929, when Willis had won both contests on points, and Casey was anxious to reverse these defeats. Willis took the first three rounds and it looked as though he was on his way to another win over Casey, until Casey nailed him, in the fourth round, and had him hanging over the ropes. Willis recovered in the fifth but Casey caught him again in the sixth, putting him down for a count of nine, and he floored him again in the eighth. The two men went at it hammer and tongs in the ninth, although Casey was clearly proving to be the stronger man and he dumped Willis on the canvas for eight in the tenth round. Willis threw in the towel at the end of the tenth and he vowed:

'I would not fight Casey again for a pound a week pension.'

Casey met Dick Bartlett, at the Borough hall, Hartlepool, on 29 June 1931, and the fight was a complete sell-out with hundreds being turned away. Bartlett was a local favourite who had been assisted in his training by Jack London and Jack Strongbow. The two men were matched at 12 stone 3lb, but Bartlett weighed in at 12 stone 9 lb which meant that Casey was conceding fully a stone in weight to his opponent, yet he readily consented to the fight going ahead. In the event, the difference in weights did not matter: Bartlett proved no match for Casey. Casey floored Bartlett in the first round, and in the second round, the Hartlepool fighter threw caution to the wind and took a mighty swipe at Casey's chin, which missed, and Casey promptly knocked him out with a right cross to the jaw.

After his string of impressive victories, Casey was given his first fight in London, and the promoter, Jeff Dickson, could not have chosen a tougher opponent: Marcel Thil, the French middleweight champion, later to become the world champion. Thil had already beaten the British middleweight champion, Len Harvey, and the British welterweight champion, Jack Hood, when he was matched with Casey. Apparently, Jeff Dickson had difficulty in finding a British boxer prepared to enter the ring against the fearsome Frenchman before he finally lined up Casey. It proved to be an inspired piece of matchmaking. Thil was completely bald but with an excess of body hair. He was a tough, dour fighter with a long string of knock-outs to his credit. Casey was paid £50 for his fight with Thil, his biggest purse to date.

The fight took place at the Royal Albert Hall, on 9 November 1931. It was Casey's first visit to London and he was determined to make the most of it. He spent the day of the fight walking round London, looking at the sights, including the Lord Mayor's Show. It was a foolish thing to do, as he realised later, and he would have been better advised to have rested up on the afternoon before his gruelling contest with Thil.

MARCEL THIL
French Middleweight Champion

Casey caused a minor sensation, in the opening round, when he split Thil's left eyebrow with a fierce right. The eye bled for five rounds and there was a strong possibility that the Frenchman might be forced to retire. The crowd began to sense that there could be an upset and urged Casey on. But Thil's handlers did a good bit of patching up on the cut and Thil began to treat Casey with more respect. In the sixth round, Thil, aware that his

18

cut eye made him vulnerable, went all out to finish the fight with a knock-out, but, in doing so, he left himself open to a Casey right smash to the jaw which shook the French champion. Over the last four rounds, Thil pulled out all the stops against the Sunderland man and he hammered his way to a points victory. After the fight, Thil described Casey as the 'toughest man in the world'.

Peter Wilson wrote that the fight was 'one of the bloodiest brawls ever seen at the only abattoir in South Kensington- the Albert Hall. For once, Thil met a man who could take it as long as he could dish it out'; and the correspondent of *Boxing* wrote:

> *'The outstanding feature of the evening without doubt was the amazing display given by Jack Casey of Sunderland against Marcel Thil, the French middleweight champion. Boxers who can absorb a more than usual amount of punishment have been likened to human blotting pads. The term is absolutely inadequate in describing Casey, he must be the whole of the blotting paper mill. Casey is no ordinary man. He took enough punches to have dropped a dozen men and Thil apparently became sick and tired of punching him before the astonishing affair terminated'.*

Casey ended the year with wins over Joe Woodruff, in three rounds, Bob McGovern, in one round, and Harry Mason, who was disqualified for holding in the third round. Nine days after the Mason fight, Casey made his second appearance in a London ring, boxing six rounds with Seaman Harvey, at Blackfriars, on the occasion of a benefit for Arthur Gutteridge, the famous second. The distance was not long enough to enable Casey to wear down the crafty sailor and he lost on points. After the fight, Casey played a mouth-organ duet with Dom Valante in the centre of the ring. Casey had some musical talent, for he could also play the piano accordion and the banjo, and he had a pleasant singing voice.

To round off what had been a momentous year for him, Casey met Billy Adair at New St James' Hall, on 28 December 1931, and forced him to retire, in the third round.

BRITISH BOXING BOARD OF CONTROL (1929)

PROMOTER AND BOXER.

ARTICLES OF AGREEMENT.
(B.B.B. of C.   Form No. 35a).

An Agreement entered into this   20th. day of OCTOBER   19 31 between

JEFF DICKSON   of   LONDON

(hereinafter called the Promoter) of the one part

And   JACK CASEY   of   SUNDERLAND

(hereinafter called the Boxer) of the other part

WHEREBY IT IS AGREED AS FOLLOWS :—

1. The Boxer agrees to appear at   THE ROYAL ALBERT HALL LONDON

on the evening/afternoon of   November 9th.   19 31 , and box
Marcel Thil   of   France   10 rounds
of 3 minutes each with an interval of one minute between each round at 11 stone 8 lbs.,
with 6 oz. gloves under National Sporting Club Boxing Rules (B.B.B.C. REG. 30). The Boxer
to weigh in at the to be named , at 2 P.M. on the day of the
contest. If over weight to forfeit the sum of £ 10 (One hour allowed to do the correct weight.)

2. The Promoter to pay the Boxer the sum of £ 50-0-0 —or——————— per cent.
of the Gross receipts if he wins the said Contest : £ 50-0-0 or per cent. of the Gross
receipts if he loses and £ 50-0-0 or per cent. of the Gross receipts if the said
Contest is drawn. (Gross receipts do not include Entertainment Tax.)

In the event of the Promoter breaking this contract he shall pay the Boxer £ 25 damages.
In the event of the Boxer breaking this contract he shall pay the Promoter £ 25 damages.

In the event of the Boxer's opponent breaking his contract, through unforeseen circumstances or
otherwise, The British Boxing Board of Control (1929), to settle any claim for compensation.

3. If by mutual agreement the Purse money is to be deposited with The British Boxing Board of Control
(1929), same must be deposited on or before the

4. The Boxer to deposit the sum of £ 25 with the Promoter as a guarantee of his
appearance and his compliance with the conditions. In the event of the Contest taking place, the sum deposited
shall be returned to the Boxer.

5. The Referee and Timekeeper shall be appointed by the Management, or mutually agreed upon, or
appointed by The British Boxing Board of Control (1929).

6. The Boxer shall not box publicly   seven   days before the date of the contest without
the consent in writing of the Promoter.

7. The Boxer to be certified in a fit condition to box by a duly qualified Medical Officer appointed
by the Promoter or The British Boxing Board of Control (1929).

8. Should the Boxer be certified or declared under Clause 7 of this Agreement, or during training,
to be unfit to box, and such unfitness is not attributable to the Boxer's own misconduct, his deposit shall
be retained by the Promoter, and the Boxer agrees not to enter into any other Agreement before he has
fulfilled a similar engagement for the Promoter.

Outstanding contracts for contests after the one mentioned herein but signed previously are allowed to
stand provided same have been reported to the Promoter before the time of such unfitness. The date of the
last contest or " when again fit " must be reported to the Promoter by the Boxer within 7 days.

The Promoter within 7 days of the date given must inform the Boxer the date of the substitute contest, a further 14 days allowed for the contest to take place.

In the event of the Promoter not giving a date to the Boxer within the 7 days allowed, the deposit shall
be returned to the Boxer and thereafter this contract shall become null and void. In the event of the substitute contest taking place in accordance with the original articles the deposit shall be returned to the Boxer.

If, however, the Boxer's condition as aforesaid is caused by the Boxer's own misconduct, then the said
deposit shall be handed to such Boxer's opponent, and such unfit Boxer shall be considered as having
broken this Contract. Should, however, both Boxers be declared unfit through their own misconduct,
the Promoter shall be entitled to the deposit and the Boxer shall be liable to pay damages, but in assessing
such damages such deposited sum shall be taken into account.

[P.T.O.

THE MOST POPULAR PRICED ENTERTAINMENT EVER
PRODUCED IN GREAT BRITAIN

ROYAL ALBERT HALL

Monday, November 9th, 1931, at 8 p.m.

Manager:
C. B. COCHRAN

JEFF DICKSON PROMOTION

Great Anglo-French Night

10 (Three-minute) Rounds Contest

NEL TARLETON

(LIVERPOOL). Feather-weight Champion of Great Britain. Now matched with Battling Battalino for the Championship of the World.

V.

NICK BENSA

(PARIS). Feather-weight Champion of France. Recently gave Al Brown a stiff battle, losing narrowly on points. Both men to weigh-in at 9st. 11lb. at 2 o'clock.

10 (Three-minute) Rounds Contest

SPIDER PLADNER

(PARIS). Bantam-weight Champion of France. Contender for the World's Championship. Recently matched with Al Brown for the Title, but Brown ran out.

V.

JOHNNY PETERS

(BATTERSEA). The ex-Schoolboy Champion who, after a brilliant run of successes in Australia and America, seems to have puzzled the referees' judgment since his return. Sure to be a champion. Both men to weigh-in at 8st. 8lb.

10 (Three-minute) Rounds Contest

MARCEL THIL

(PARIS.) Middle-weight Champion of France and Contender for the World's Championship. Recently defeated Vince Dundee.

V.

JACK CASEY

(SUNDERLAND). Known as the Sunderland Assassin. Gave Jack Hood a terrific fight over Fifteen Rounds, losing narrowly on points. One of the most promising of the younger middle-weights. Both men to weigh-in at 11st. 8lb, at 2 o'clock.

10 (Three-minute) Rounds Return Contest

FREDDIE WEBSTER

(KENTISH TOWN.) Recently defeated Harry Mason. Has now got substantial backing to meet Kid Berg.

V.

EUGENE DROUHIN

(FRANCE.) Known as the K.O. King. Early this year met Webster in this hall, and after one of the best fights seen here the contest was declared a draw, hence this return.

POPULAR PUBLIC PRICES (including tax)

GALLERY.	BALCONY.	BOXES AND ORCH.	LOWER ORCH.	LOGGIAS.	STALLS.	RINGSIDE.
3/6	8/6	12/-	15/-	18/-	21/-	24/-

Seats can be booked at the Royal Albert Hall and a Messrs. Keith Prowse, Alfred Hays District Messengers, Webster and Waddington, Webster and Girling, and all Agencies; Sid Parsons, 56, Farringdon Road, E.C. (Holborn 7210); Jeff Dickson's Offices, 8 and 10, Cecil Court, Charing Cross Road W.C.2 (Temple Bar 5523 and 8922). BIRMINGHAM: Jim Murphy, Farcroft Hotel, Rookery Road, Handsworth (Northorn 0657).

21

After the Thil Fight. Cartoon from London **Evening News** *10 November 1931*

Chapter 5

FIGHTING FOR THE CHAMPIONSHIP

Casey started 1932 with a return match, on 18 January 1932, against Dick Bartlett, at Manchester. The fight had been arranged at Bartlett's request because he had been dissatisfied with his performance in his previous outing against Casey, six months before, and believed that he would do better second time round. But the result was the same: Casey knocked him out in the second round. 'Give me no more of Casey', said Bartlett, after the fight, 'I'd sooner fight Primo Carnera'.

Jack Casey was now at the peak of his fighting form and Walter Russell had taken over as his manager. John Paget, the promoter and owner of New St James' Hall, was anxious to give Casey a chance of fighting for the British middleweight championship, then held by Len Harvey. Paget had secured Harvey's agreement to fight Casey at Newcastle, but the British Boxing Board of Control refused to sanction the match as a championship fight. The Board gave no reason for its decision but perhaps it considered Casey's claims to be inferior to those of Jock McAvoy and Archie Sexton, the two other main contenders for the title. Nevertheless, the fight went ahead, as a fifteen round non-championship bout, on 8 February 1932. It was, of course, a sell-out and the famous 'graveyard of champions' was packed to the rafters with excited fans. Most of the crowd were from the Tyne and Wear area, and they had come to see if Len Harvey, arguably Britain's most accomplished boxer of the inter-war years, would fall to the fists of their local hero.

Casey took the fight to Harvey from the opening bell, forcing the champion to do a bit of back-pedalling, to avoid his opponent's rushes. Early on in the fight, a Casey right-hand punch caught Harvey on his left arm and sent him sprawling into the ropes, but the champion was unhurt and retaliated by pounding Casey's body. Midway through the fourth round, Harvey caught Casey with two of his best punches. In Peter Wilson's words: "Harvey had a wicked left-hook to the body and a right to the jaw which only ferro-concrete buildings masqerading as men- like 'cast-iron' Casey- could sustain without collapsing into ruins." The punches put Casey on the canvas but he was up immediately and continued to carry the fight to Harvey. After his failure to finish the fight by a knock-out, Harvey resorted to a more defensive approach. He jabbed with his left, smothered Casey's fierce attacks by holding, and did some body pummelling when he could. The crowd roared its disapproval of Harvey's 'spoiling' tactics, but the champion was unperturbed and he continued to jab and smother until the last two rounds, when he opened up again on Casey. At the end of the fifteen rounds, Harvey was awarded the victory on points. Some local fans howled their disagreement with the decision, but most objective observers recognised that Harvey, a master boxer, had cleverly built up a clear points lead over his more aggressive opponent.

After the fight, Harvey paid a visit to Casey's dressing-room.

> *"You are a great boxer." said Jack, in admiration.*
> *"I have to be against men like you, " replied the champion.*
> *"What do they feed you on- iron filings?"*
> *"Will you give me another fight?" asked Casey.*
> *"Of course, any time you like." replied Harvey.*

However, it was Jock McAvoy who got the next middleweight championship fight with Harvey, at Manchester, on 21 March 1932; and, after McAvoy's defeat, the Board of Control ruled that McAvoy must defend his Northern Area middleweight title against Casey, the winner to meet Archie Sexton for the right to challenge Harvey for the title. John Paget tried to get the McAvoy-Casey fight for New St James' Hall but was outbid by the Belle Vue syndicate and the fight took place at Manchester, on 18 July 1932.

In between the Harvey and McAvoy fights, Casey scored nine consecutive wins, disposing of Seaman Harvey, Sandy McKenzie, Jack Marshall, Hal O'Neill, Red Pullen, Les Saunders, Glen Moody, Eddie Strawer and Billy Thomas, and there were few who doubted that he had earned the right to challenge McAvoy for the Northern Area middleweight title.

RED PULLEN
Welsh middleweight

Jock McAvoy, the 'Rochdale Thunderbolt', was an aggressive two-handed fighter with many knock-outs to his credit, but he knew Casey's reputation and chose to follow hit and run tactics when they met. Casey had to do the chasing, while McAvoy built up a comfortable points lead with his counter punching. McAvoy appeared to be in control of the fight until the eleventh round when Casey caught him with a left hook that sent McAvoy's gum-shield spinning across the ring. Casey continued to bore in during the twelfth round, and there was some wild punching from both men. McAvoy slung a low blow at Casey's body and was warned by the referee to keep his punches up. In round thirteen, Casey caught McAvoy with a vicious upper-cut which, according to one observer, 'lifted McAvoy off the boards'. The Rochdale man was badly shaken and, although McAvoy was still well ahead on points, it was Casey who looked the fresher of the two when they returned to their corners at the end of the round. The fourteenth proved to be the last round. McAvoy put Casey on the canvas with a blow to the body. There was an appeal for a foul from Casey's corner but the referee, Tom Gamble, ignored it. Casey rose and McAvoy launched another right to the body which caused Casey to curl up in agony, and this time the referee stepped between the two men to award the fight to Casey, on a disqualification.

After the fight, McAvoy commented:

> *'I wondered if I might be the first man to do what every other Casey opponent had failed to do, and stick Jack on the canvas for ten seconds. I had every reason to think I could beat the Sunderland Assassin. That I failed, was just hard luck. To tell the truth, I had got tired of hitting Jack on the chin with punches which would have knocked out any ordinary scrapper cold, so I switched my attack to the solar-plexus. It was a complete surprise to me after the referee decided to rule me out, because he had not warned me for the punches which dropped Casey on the first occasion, and which he obviously considered legitimate.'*

Casey's version was that McAvoy was so dazed by the upper-cut which rocked him in the thirteenth round, that his judgement had become faulty and he had strayed below the belt with his body punches.

Few people knew that Jack Casey had had very little sleep before his fight with McAvoy. He had stayed the night at his uncle's home, in Ashton-under-Lyne, and had retired to bed early enough, but had been woken up by the arrival of a crowd of North Eastern supporters who had come to wish him luck. Hearing the noise, Jack Casey dressed and went down to meet them, and there was no more sleep for him that night. It was scarcely the best preparation for a major fight, but Casey never complained about it.

Casey was due to travel back to Sunderland the day after the fight and a brass band had been arranged to meet him at the railway station on his return. When Jack learned of these preparations, he altered his arrangements, leaving the train at West Hartlepool and travelling the remainder of the distance by road to Sunderland. He then made his way quietly through the back streets of the town to his home in the East End, where he went straight to bed to catch up on his sleep.

After his defeat of McAvoy, the Board of Control ruled that Casey should meet Archie Sexton, in a final eliminator for Harvey's British middleweight title. Casey and Sexton had met three times previously, at Sunderland, Manchester and South Shields. The score was one win each and a draw. The fight took place at New St James' Hall, on 3 October 1932. Both men boxed cautiously until round seven, when Casey launched a whirlwind of punches at Sexton: a left jab to the nose was followed by a right to Sexton's temple and a left hook to the jaw. Sexton went down, blinded by pain and tears, and was counted out, holding his right glove over his eyes. This was a vintage Casey performance and it earned him the coveted championship match with Harvey.

Efforts were made to stage the championship fight in Casey's home town, and the *Regal* cinema and the *Empire* theatre were mooted as possible venues, but the match went to purse offers and John Paget secured it for New St James' Hall, to take place on 12 December 1932. Casey was not unhappy with this outcome because he regarded 'St Jim's' as having been a lucky stadium for him in the past and he liked boxing there. He

Jack Casey and sparring partners.
left to right: Joe Woodruff, Frank Bagley,
Jack Casey and Gunner Ainsley

was not without his superstitions and he always wore a sprig of heather in the lapel of his coat when entering a boxing stadium.

In his championship preparations, Casey was assisted by Frank Bagley, Joe Woodruff, George Willis and Gunner Ainsley who acted as his chief sparring partners; and he fitted in three fights: he out-pointed the ex-policeman, George Brown, on points over twelve rounds at Leeds; he knocked out Canadian middleweight, Del Fontaine, in the fourth round, at New St James' Hall; and forced Glen Moody, the Welsh middleweight champion, to retire in the third round, at the same venue.

Jack Casey spars with
George Willis in preparation
for the Harvey fight

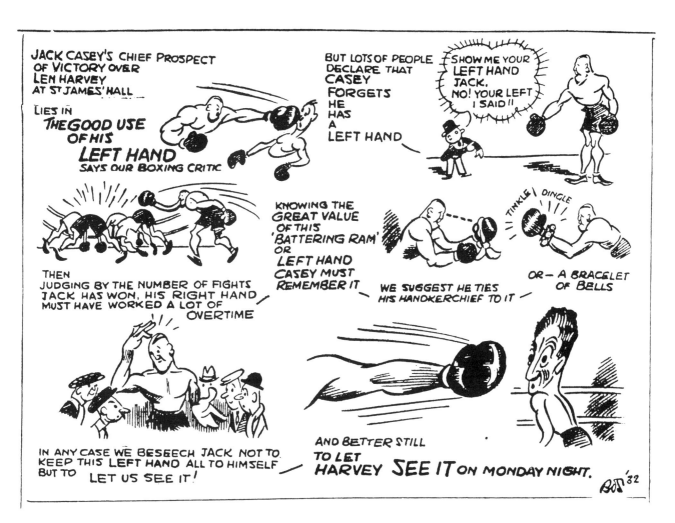

Some advice to Jack Casey.
Cartoon from Evening Chronicle 12 December 1932

The referee for the championship fight was Arthur S. Myers and, in the first round, he made it clear to Len Harvey that he would not stand for the excessive holding which had marred the first contest between the two men, and, to be fair to Harvey, he did his best to make it a clean and open contest.

Casey forced the pace from the opening bell, but not with his usual wild rushes. He fought with great skill and Harvey realised how much Casey had improved since their earlier meeting, ten months before. The first five rounds were fairly even, then, in the sixth round, Casey, in a flurry of punches, caught Harvey with a hard right to the jaw. Harvey was hurt and fell back on the ropes, with his arms dangling by his sides. The crowd went wild with excitement. To many people in the hall, Harvey looked to be out on his feet and that it needed only one good punch to finish him off. But Casey hesitated and drew back. One story is that someone from Casey's corner shouted: 'Watch him, Jack, he's foxing.' Harvey had gained a vital respite and he slid off the ropes and out of danger.

Several years later, Harvey gave his version of the incident in a newspaper article:

*"I was three parts out and in a dazed, muzzy sort of fashion
I could see Casey ready to step in and finish me. The
obvious thing to do was to cover up but had I done that I
should never have lasted to the end of the round. Instead, I
took a big chance- and it came off. I let my arms hang limp
over the top rope, and there I sagged like a sack of potatoes,
watching Jack through half-closed eyes. I saw a shadow of
bewilderment cross his face and he drew back. Three . . four
. . five seconds passed and all the time the crowd were yelling
themselves hoarse with excitement.
'Go on, Jack,' they shouted, 'Go in and finish him.' but
Casey suspected a trap; he had heard tales that I was most
dangerous when I was apparently almost out- and so he held
off and lost the fight."*

The sixth round was a bad round for Harvey in another respect: he had injured his right
hand on Casey's jaw, which he likened to hitting a brick wall, and for the remainder of
the fight he had to be careful how he used it.

Casey's aggression won him the middle rounds, but Harvey began to look stronger in the
ninth, tenth and eleventh rounds, then halfway through the twelfth round Casey caught
Harvey with a hard right, flush on the jaw, which sent him staggering back on the ropes.
As Casey prepared to move in, Harvey gave a faint smile, some observers say he
winked, and Casey hesitated for crucial seconds which enabled the champion to clear
his brain and slide off the ropes to the safety of the open ring.

In the last four rounds, Harvey showed true championship class. He was noted for his
ability to pace a fight and he knew exactly what he had to do to win this one. Casey
continued to battle gamely until the final bell, however the punches he had taken from
Harvey began to slow him down in the later rounds, whereas Harvey seemed to be able
to draw upon fresh sources of stamina. The champion won the last four rounds- although
Casey clipped him with a good right hand in the fourteenth round- and boxed a brilliant
final round to clinch the fight.

The referee therefore awarded the final verdict to Len Harvey, and Lord Tweedsmouth,
deputising for Lord Lonsdale, placed the Lonsdale Belt around the champion's waist.
The decision, by common agreement, was a close one, but, most observers felt the
referee's verdict was correct. 'Argus', sports' correspondent of the *Sunderland Echo*,
summed it up:

> *'Harvey was entitled to the verdict. There was not a great
> deal in it, but what there was, was brought about by superior
> ring-craft. Harvey used the ring better. He used his cunning
> too, and he was not so clean a fighter as Casey.'*

One dissenter was Jim Ainsley, one of Casey's sparring partners, who witnessed the fight.
Recalling the event, thirty years later, the old Gunner observed:

'I was always a great admirer of Harvey, but I still consider Len was lucky to beat Jack Casey for the British middleweight title. As a matter of fact, if I had been the referee, I would have awarded Casey the fight on points because of his better boxing up to the eleventh round. Len won the last four rounds but, in my book, this was not enough.'

In reporting the fight, Fred Charlton believed that the sixth round was the crucial one when Casey allowed it to slip away, whereas the boxing correspondent, Gilbert Odd, thought the twelfth round was the decisive one, when Harvey 'foxed' his way out of trouble with a smile.

Jack Casey poses with his piano accordian during a break from training for the Harvey championship fight. His son, John, stands beside him in the ring.

When Harvey looked back on the fight later in life, he observed with a twinkle in his eye: 'Don't talk to me about that fellow Casey. I should have known better than to fight him the first time; I should have had my brains tested for taking him on again.' He said that his championship fight with Casey had been the hardest of his boxing career; and he told Henry Cooper that his right hand had never been the same since he had cracked it on Casey's jaw. Jack Casey took his defeat philosophically, and spent the next day relaxing at home, playing his piano accordion.

At the weigh-in of the British Middleweight Championship figt 12 December 1932. left to right : C.Rose (Harvey's manager), Len Harvey, Mr J. J. Paget the promoter, Jack Casey, and Mr C.F.Donmall, Secretary of the British Board of Control.

Lord Tweedmouth presents the Lonsdale Belt to Len Harvey after the successful defence of his middleweight title.

Chapter 6

MARKING TIME

The Harvey fight put Jack Casey at the peak of his fame and popularity in his home town. The contraction of the ship-building industry in the 1920's had hit Sunderland hard, but the onset of the world depression in 1929 considerably worsened the town's economic plight. In 1931, there were 24,163 men unemployed in the town, representing 36.6 per cent of its male working population, and unemployment continued to rise until it peaked, at 29,071, in 1934. These were grim years for many Sunderland families and their lives were brightened up by Jack Casey's exploits in the ring. His fights were followed avidly in the local press, and he was idolised wherever he went. A local artist painted his portrait in oils and Jack had the painting on public display in the front room window of his house.

Casey now had his own gymnasium in a large upper room of the Golden Lion Hotel in High Street East (a move from cramped training premises in Moss Lane) which was also the home of the Jack Casey school of boxing. The school, managed by Jack's father, developed local boxing talent and provided promoters with fighters for their bills. Jack Clansey, Al White and Arthur Clarey (Jack's younger brother) were among the graduates of this school.

Jack Casey was now earning big money by the standards of the time, and he was extremely generous with it. After the Harvey fight, he arranged a Christmas party for the children of the town's East End. He gave generously to the Mayor's boot fund for poor children and, if he saw a child going barefoot in the street, he would put his hand in his pocket and give its mother the price of a new pair of shoes. In the pubs he frequented, it was a case of ' the drinks are on Jack Casey'.

The fight with Len Harvey for the British middleweight championship had also put Jack Casey at the peak of his boxing career, and there were several options open to him. Casey wanted a return bout with Harvey, although he conceded that he would probably have to fight an eliminating contest with Jock McAvoy before he got another shot at the British middleweight title. There were also negotiations underway which would put Casey into the ring with Marcel Thil for the world middleweight championship. After the excitement generated by their first clash this would have proved a sure-fire money spinner, as the promoters well knew, and would have been a much more attractive proposition than another Thil-Harvey meeting. Casey was also in touch with Charlie Harvey, who handled the contracts for British boxers fighting in the United States. The Americans were very keen to see Casey in action in their rings, and Harvey was confident he could line up a number of lucrative matches. After the Harvey fight, Casey said he would wait to see what came of the negotiations for a fight with Thil, then, in March 1933, he hoped to go to America for a few fights, and, by the time he returned from the States, the position concerning the British middleweight championship should have been sorted out by the Board of Control, and Casey was confident he would be involved in their plans.

In the event, none of these things happened. There was no return contest with Thil,

BELLE VUE BOXING GAZETTE

SECOND CONTEST

Twelve Three-Minutes Rounds Contest

JACK CASEY v. PAUL SCHAEFER

Weigh in at 11 st. 8 lbs.

JACK CASEY

(Sunderland). Official Middle-weight (11 st. 6 lbs.) Champion of the North of England, who is now back in his best form.

Result ....

PAUL SCHAEFER

(Canada) who has K.O. the best men in America, including Tommy Wilson, Frank Roddy, Billy Neath, Phil Rocks, Lex Kemp, Jimmy Murphy, Judd Eadis, Eddie Walsh, and K.O. Reggie Perkins (London) who recently defeated Jack Casey.

4

Programme : Belle Vue Stadium 23 October 1933

Casey did not go to America, and McAvoy was given the next championship fight with Harvey. For the next two years, Casey's career not so much declined as drifted. He was still a top of the bill attraction to the boxing public and good enough to score some notable victories over first class fighters, but his career lacked direction. He fought too often and did not pick his fights carefully enough, being prepared to fight anybody, anywhere, at any weight, and this included heavyweights. In 1933, he was still one of the country's leading middleweight contenders and his main objective should have been to challenge for the British middleweight title. A few well-chosen fights against top middleweight opposition, with Casey trained to his peak of fitness, would have made more sense than fighting every fortnight against anybody prepared to climb into the ring with him.

In Casey's defence, he was now a family man. His son, John, was born in 1930 and his second son, George, was born in 1932. Casey said that he intended to provide for them as well as he could, and, as a professional boxer, this could only be done by entering the ring. This was a laudable enough objective but did Casey set about achieving it in the right way? Did it make sense to accept every fight offer that came along? Casey had been paid £851 for his championship fight with Len Harvey. This was the biggest purse of his career at a time when he was being paid £20-£25 for topping the bill at provincial halls in non-title fights. Fighting for quick money returns was a short-sighted policy for Casey to follow: it harmed his career 1933-34 and, in the long run, it damaged his health.

Casey was also ill-advised to neglect the London rings, where the boxing correspondents on the national newspapers picked up most of the copy for their columns. Casey's first appearance in a London ring- against Marcel Thil- had been little short of sensational, yet Casey had followed it up by fighting only once more in London, in a six round contest on a charity bill. From the point of view of earning money, Casey did not need to fight in London. Northern promoters were only too happy to have him on their bills, and Casey was content to fight in familiar rings for promoters he knew and liked. Fighting in London also involved additional travelling and the costs of overnight accommodation. Yet, a few fights in London would have enhanced his reputation in the capital, where many of the important decisions were taken, and kept his name in the national newspapers.

Len Harvey took a three months rest after the championship fight, nursing his injured hand, but, within a month, Casey was in action again, beating Eddie Maguire, the South African middleweight champion, on points over twelve rounds at New St James' Hall. A fortnight later, he defeated Seaman Harvey on points over fifteen rounds at Plymouth; and, a fortnight after this, he forced Leo Bandias, the Australian light heavyweight champion, to retire in the twelfth round, at New St James' Hall. On 6 February 1933, Casey met Maguire in a re-match at Newcastle. In the third round, the referee stepped in to part them from a clinch and Maguire dropped his guard. Casey was in like a flash with his right and Maguire went down for the full count. A re-match was made on the spot and the pair met, a fortnight later, when Maguire, keeping the fight at long range, boxed his way to a points victory over twelve rounds. In between his fights with Maguire, Casey disposed of Eddie Robinson in four rounds at Liverpool. This meant that Casey had fought six contests in 63 days.

LIVERPOOL STADIUM (Adjoining EXCHANGE STATION)

THE FINEST BOXING HALL IN GREAT BRITAIN

TO=MORROW, THURSDAY, MARCH 9th, at 7.45 LIVERPOOL STADIUM LTD., PRESENT
(Under the Direction of Johnny Best)

TWELVE Three-Minute Rounds Middle-weight Contest at 11st. 10lb. Weigh in at 2 p.m

JACK CASEY v. EDDIE ROBINSON

Sunderland, recently boxed Len Harvey for the Middle-weight Title and Belt. **Birmingham,** has boxed a draw with Casey.

TWELVE Three-Minute Rounds Contest at 9st. 10lb.

FRED TILSTON Chester v. BOYO REES Wales

TEN Three-Minute Rounds Contest

JIMMY WALSH Chester v. TOM BAILEY Liverpool

TEN Three-Minute Rounds Contest

JOE CURRAN Liverpool v. PHIL MILLIGAN Oldham

Also Other Contests. Ladies Admitted.

Tickets Obtained at:—STADIUM (Telephone: Bank 4727);
JACK SHARP, Whitechapel; RUSHWORTH & DREAPER, Islington; PIED BULL HOTEL Chester.

RESERVED. All Bookable Seats.

Prices of Admission (including Tax)	Ringside	Extension	Circle	Outer Circle	Unreserved
	7/6	**5/-**	**3/6**	**2/6**	**1/6**

His next fight was a twelve round contest against his old rival, Archie Sexton, at Belle Vue, on 10 April 1933, as the chief supporting bout to the Harvey-McAvoy British middleweight championship fight. The promoters had put the country's four top middleweights on the same bill. This time, Sexton gave Casey a good pasting and won a points victory over the cast iron man. The result undoubtedly influenced the Boxing Board of Control in their decision to name Sexton as the main contender to meet the new champion, Jock McAvoy, for the British middleweight title. In effect, if not in name, the Casey-Sexton fight was a final eliminator for the British middleweight championship, and, if Casey had beaten Sexton, he would surely have gained a second chance to fight for the title. Sexton won and went on to fight McAvoy for the title, in October 1933. It is difficult not to conclude that if Casey had had fewer fights in the run-up to the Belle Vue contest and had made some special preparations for the Sexton fight, he would have performed better and perhaps have beaten Sexton. After all, he had stopped Sexton twice within the distance at their previous meetings, and another victory over the Londoner was not out of the question. As it was, Casey had missed a golden opportunity of establishing his claim to be the leading contender for McAvoy's title.

After the Sexton fight, Casey continued with his fight-a-fortnight programme, beating Joe Woodruff in six rounds, Les Ward in seven, and going to Paris to meet Carmelo Candel. Candel was a Frenchman from Oran in Algeria. He had been Marcel Thil's sparring partner and his ambition was to follow in Thil's footsteps by winning the French, European and World middleweight titles. Casey went to Paris with a big reputation. The French boxing fans knew him as the tough Englishman who had nearly caused a major upset in his London fight with Marcel Thil. They were, however, disappointed by his performance against Candel. A jaded Casey had little to offer but his toughness, and he retired at the end of the fifth round, with a battered face and a badly cut eye, having barely laid a glove on his opponent. It was the Sexton fight all over again and the lesson to Casey was clear: he could not hope to be at his best against top class fighters when he was fighting every fortnight. Yet, eleven days later, Casey was fighting in Scotland and in devastating form against Dino Guselli, forcing the Italian to retire at the end of the second round.

Ten days after this, Casey stepped into the ring with Jack London, in an open-air contest, at the Engineers' Club, in West Hartlepool. Jack London- a future British and Empire heavyweight champion- was then an up and coming heavyweight of twenty years of age. He was young but no novice. He had 41 fights under his belt and was on a winning streak, having gone his previous eleven fights without a defeat. He had beaten such useful heavies as Tony Arpino, Al Conquest, Battling Sullivan, Bert Ikin, Gunner Ainsley, and Bill Brennan. London was big and strong with a left jab like a battering ram and a piledriver of a right hand. Casey weighed in at 12 stone, conceding two stones plus height and reach to London.

The promoters knew that the match would be a sell-out. Jack London was a local lad and Casey had been a popular performer in Hartlepool rings over the years. A win over Jack Casey would look good in Jack London's record, but what did Casey hope to gain by agreeing to the match? Apparently, it was the appeal of money. Jack was planning a Mediterranean cruise, in July, and was tempted by the big purse offer. Casey was a very popular figure on leisure cruises. He used to do a bit of exhibition boxing on deck, and in the evenings he entertained his fellow passengers with tunes on his piano accordion.

The fight took place in pouring rain, although the capacity crowd of 3,000 sat it out to the last punch. Casey opened in whirlwind fashion, going for a quick knock-out, but London beat off the early attacks of the shorter man and, thereafter, it was London all the way, as he bounced punches off Casey's jaw almost at will. Casey hit the canvas in the fourth round, but was up without a count and he never gave up throwing punches. But, as the blows rained down on him and Casey hit the deck again in the tenth round, the crowd began to wonder if London might prove to be the first man to knock out 'cast-iron' Casey.

Then, in the interval between rounds ten and eleven, London announced his retirement due to a damaged right hand. It was a sensational end to the fight. Some criticised London's decision to withdraw when he was so far ahead on points and with Casey looking well beaten. But, there were still five rounds to go and time enough for the Assassin to 'stick one on' his young opponent. London felt that he could not carry on with an injured hand and the decision went to Casey. A fortnight later, Casey fitted in another fight- losing on points to Ernie Simmons at Leicester- before setting off on his summer cruise.

As Casey set off for the Mediterranean, *Boxing* magazine published its ratings of British boxers. In the middleweight division, Jock McAvoy as champion was rated number one, and Archie Sexton was listed as main contender. Len Harvey (asssuming he could make the weight and wished to continue to fight as a middleweight) was rated next, and Jack Casey was rated number four, with Tommy Moore as number five and George Brown number six. In spite of some poor performances in the first half of 1933, Casey was still rated in the top four of British middleweights. He was still Northern area middleweight champion and several promoters were interested in matching Casey with Tommy Moore of Royston in a Northern Area title fight. Both Casey and Moore were agreeable to the match, but the Board of Control declined to give its approval to a title fight between the two men, and, as it turned out, Casey never defended the Northern Area middleweight championship he had won by defeating Jock McAvoy, in 1932.

After a six week break, Casey returned to the ring, in a match against Carlisle's Billy Wallace, at the Engineers' Club, Darlington. Wallace was outclassed and the referee stopped the contest in the third round. A week later, however, there was a real upset when Reg Perkins of Bedford outpointed Casey over twelve rounds, at the Middlesbrough National Sporting Club. Perkins was a crafty spoiler and he cleverly edged his way to a points win over Casey; and, a fortnight later, Ernie Simmons also outpointed Casey, over twelve rounds, at Hartlepool. *Boxing* magazine commented on Casey's decline since his championship fight with Harvey and wondered ' has the pitcher been taken to the well too often?'

Casey came back after these two defeats to beat Johnny Summers, Paul Schaeffer and Andy McLaughlin; and ended the year by drawing with Eddie Maguire, over fifteen rounds, at Hull. In the December edition, *Boxing* published its end of the year middleweight ratings:
1. Jock McAvoy (British middleweight champion) 2. Archie Sexton 3. Jack Ellis
4. Seaman Wakelin 5. Ted Shaw 6. Ernie Simmons 7. Jack Casey
8. Tommy Moore 9. George Gordon 10. Jack Hyams
Casey was still rated in the top ten of British middleweights, but he had dropped to number seven in the rankings.

Douglas Parker and Jack Casey, with their piano accordians, entertain children
at an East End Christmas party held in December 1933.

Chapter 7

CRUISERS AND HEAVYWEIGHTS

In 1934, Casey relinquished his Northern Area middleweight title because he was no longer able to make the 11 stone 6lb weight limit and, from then on, he fought as a cruiserweight. Weighing in at 12 stone, he produced some of his best form and began to emerge as one of the leading contenders for the British light heavyweight title. He scored victories over Johnny Summers (in a return match), Les Ward, Bushman Dempster and Jack Marshall; and, on 19 March 1934, he faced Reggie Meen, the former British heavyweight champion, at New St James' Hall. This fight against a much bigger opponent turned out to be one of Casey's most impressive giant-killing performances. He put Meen down for a count of nine in the second round. Meen split Casey's eye in the third, but with blood streaming down his face, Casey carried the fight to the bigger man and Meen was disqualified for holding, in the fifth round. Casey then beat Dave Sullivan, in two rounds; Charlie Berlanger, the Canadian light heavyweight champion, on a disqualification in round nine; and outpointed Tommy Farr, the Welsh light heavyweight champion, over twelve rounds at New St James' Hall, on 23 April 1934.

Casey's fight with Farr was a hard and interesting contest. Casey treated Farr with great respect and adopted the tactics he had used in his fights with Len Harvey: employing boxing skill and ringcraft as well as toughness and hard punching against his opponent. The victory over Farr prompted *Boxing* magazine to comment that Casey 'was coming back into the limelight'. Casey completed a winning streak of nine consecutive victories by outpointing George Slack, the Northern Area heavyweight champion, over ten rounds. The stockily-built Slack had no counter to Casey's left jab, which, according to a local reporter, earned Casey a 'meritorious win'.

These results show that Casey was far from being on a downward slide in 1934, and if he had spaced his fights better and confined himself to fighting men of his own weight, he might yet have been given the chance of fighting for the British light heavyweight title, relinquished by Len Harvey, in June 1934.

Casey's Indian summer ended with three consecutive defeats. He lost on points to the German heavyweight, Erich Seelig, over twelve rounds; he was beaten on points by the Canadian, Paul Schaeffer, over twelve rounds; and was defeated by the promising black heavyweight from Edinburgh, Manuel Abrew, also on points over twelve rounds. Casey came back with victories over Jack Sharkey, Bushman Dempster (twice), Phil Munro, and Ginger Hauxwell.

Casey ended 1934 with fights against two top-class opponents and proved that even in defeat he was still a crowd pleaser. On 5 December, he met Leonard Steyaert, the light heavyweight champion of Belgium, at York. Casey was beaten on points over twelve rounds, in a fight which the local fans claimed was the best to have been staged in the city. The Belgian was a tall cruiserweight, with a fast left hand, which he used to pile up points in the early rounds. However, in the middle rounds, he tried to mix it with Casey, trading punch for punch, and came off worst in these exchanges. In the closing rounds,

JIMMY TARANTE
American Light Heavyweight

1934

BUSHMAN DEMPSTER
from Lanark

TOMMY FARR
Welsh Light Heavyweight Champion

CHARLIE BELANGER
Canadian Light Heavyweight Champion

he wisely resorted to his earlier tactics of keeping the fight at long range and thereby gained a points win.

A fortnight later, Casey faced the American light heavyweight, Jimmy Tarante, at New St James' Hall. Tarante was of negro and Cherokee Indian ancestry. He had been fighting for over five years in America and came to Europe with an unbeaten record. He was a ferocious body puncher and had already beaten Eddie Phillips, and, earlier in the year, had fought Len Harvey, when he had been disqualified for hitting below the belt. The boxing correspondents were in no doubt that he would have little trouble in beating Casey. But they were wrong. Tarante started well and got in some telling blows to Casey's body, but in the seventh round, Casey caught him with a hard right, followed by a left hook, which dumped the American on the canvas for a count of nine. Tarante picked himself off the floor to box defensively for the next five rounds and win the decision on points. Those who had seen Casey in his prime claimed that the Assassin of 1931-32 vintage would have finished off Tarante in the seventh round. Be that as it may, Casey had done well- much better than many expected- against a highly-rated opponent.

Over the October and December months, however, Tommy Farr, after a year of patchy performances, had chalked up wins over Seaman Harvey, Eddie Peirce and Pat Aucliffe, and the Board of Control decreed that Farr should meet Eddie Phillips for the vacant British light heavyweight title. Taking into consideration that Casey had beaten Farr in April 1934 and that Farr had lost three fights after this, including an eliminator with Eddie Phillips, if Casey had put together a winning sequence in the the closing months of the year, it would have been difficult for the Board to have denied him the title fight with Phillips. Casey wrote a letter to *Boxing* magazine, complaining about the Board's decision, but there was nothing more he could do about it. He had lost his last chance of a second title fight.

In 1935, it was back to the heavyweights. On 21 January 1935, Casey fought Charlie Smith, the young Deptford giant. Casey put Smith down for a count of nine in the third round, but the bell rang to prevent Casey from following up his

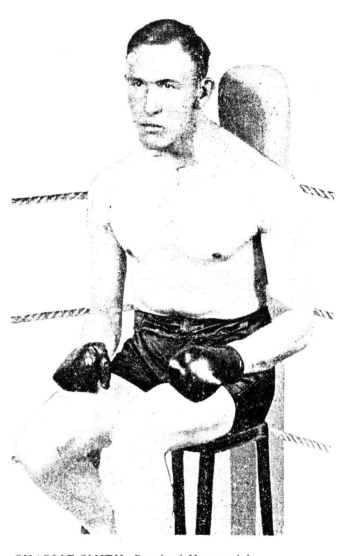

CHARLIE SMITH Deptford Heavyweight

advantage. Smith boxed more defensively after this and Casey sustained a badly cut eye which forced his retirement in round seven.

Casey's eye injury kept him out of the ring for ten weeks, and he came back matched against another heavyweight, Helmuth Hartkopp, from Germany. Again Casey dropped his opponent for a count of nine, this time in the first round, but Hartkopp was too big and strong for Casey, and the German took the decision on points.

These two punishing defeats at the hands of heavyweight opponents should have proved to Casey the folly of taking on men from the heavier division, but then he was tempted by a good offer from Jack McBeth, matchmaker for the 'Royal' stadium in Sunderland. Would Casey be interested in a return match with Jack London? The money was right so Casey agreed to meet the West Hartlepool heavyweight.

The match was a sell-out and it was a sympathetic crowd which watched Casey climb into the ring at the 'Royal', in Bedford Street. Could he pull something out of the bag against an improved boxer he had been lucky to beat two years before? The answer was 'no'. London, with a two stone weight advantage, was in top form and he punched his way to a one-sided points victory over twelve rounds. Casey at least had the consolation of lasting the distance with London. Few other boxers could have stood up to the punishment he took that night. Whatever else he had lost, he was still 'cast-iron' Casey.

JACK LONDON
West Hartlepool heavyweight

In her book on boxing, *The Ignoble Art* (1956), Edith Summerskill says of Casey's first fight with Harvey: "That terrible fight left its mark. One more terrific but unsuccessful encounter with Harvey altered the career of the 'Sunderland Assassin'." When Casey fought Harvey, he was young, fit and strong, and evenly matched against a man of the same weight. Casey's two fights with Harvey were both gruelling encounters but, in no sense, 'blood baths'. Harvey was a master of the art of self-defence and, by no means, a killer in the ring. It is doubtful if his fights with Harvey did Casey any irreparable harm and they did not end his ring career. Casey's contests against heavyweights were another matter, and it is almost certain that it was in these fights that Casey suffered the damage to brain and body which affected him later in life. The hammering he had taken from Jack London finally convinced Casey that the time had come to retire from boxing.

41

MANUEL ABREW
black heavyweight from Edinburgh

1934

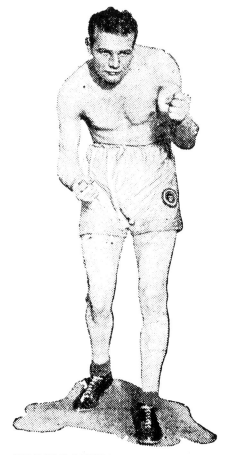

REGGIE MEEN
former British Heavyweight Champion

GEORGE SLACK
Northern Area Heavyweight Champion

42

When he got home after the fight, Casey got on to the 'phone to Fred Charlton, the boxing promoter and referee.

> " Mr Charlton," he said, "I'm quitting the game. Can you get
> me a job outside of boxing?"
> "What kind of job?"
> "A publican's job." replied Jack.

So Fred Charlton used his contacts and Jack was made landlord of Polly's Tavern, in Lambton Street, only a hundred yards from the 'Royal' where the town's boxing matches were staged. The little pub did good trade, especially on fight nights. Jovial Jack was a popular host. He entertained the customers with tunes on his piano accordion and led them in the choruses of popular songs. However, he was not a great success as the manager of a business and, eighteen months after his clash with Jack London, Casey was back in the ring.

*Polly's Tavern in Lambton Street
where Jack Casey was landlord 1935-37*

He was then twenty-nine years old. Not very old as boxers go, but few boxers had soaked up as much punishment and his style of fighting relied on strength and aggression. In 1936, he had moved from the East End of the town to a semi-detached house in Side Cliff Road, in the Fulwell area, a short walk from the sea-front, where he now did his road work and went swimming in the North Sea. 'They never come back' is an old saying in the fight game, and there are few exceptions to the general rule. Jack Casey, unfortunately, was not one of them.

The first fight in his come-back campaign was against Jackie Moran, at New St James' Hall, on 6 December 1937. Moran was an engine driver from Carlisle and the match was intended to serve as a warm-up fight for Casey. It did not turn out that way. Casey weighed in at 13 stone 1lb, a stone above his pre-retirement fighting weight, and a local boxing reporter observed: 'His long lay-off has not impaired his indomitable spirit and willingness to take punishment, but the crowd waited in vain for the dynamic rallies of old. Casey's spirit was willing but the flesh would not respond. He had the desire to start action but simply could not bring it into operation.' Moran's left hand was never out of Casey's face and he won a comfortable points victory over ten rounds.

A fortnight later, Casey faced Reggie Meen at the same venue. This time, Casey won, the referee stopping the contest in the second round. But, what was the victory worth? One observer described both men as 'being mere shadows of their former selves.' Three weeks later, Casey beat Ron Linley, at Bournemouth, the referee stopping the contest in the fifth round, and this proved to be the last win of Casey's boxing career. He had four more fights that year, against up and coming heavyweights, and lost them all. Casey lost on points over ten rounds to Stan Kirby, at Darlington; to Jim McKenzie, over ten rounds, at Newcastle; to Zachy Nicholas, over ten rounds, at Penzance; and, on 6 April 1938, Casey was forced to retire in the third round against Canadian fighter, Packy Paul, at Sheffield. He then hung up his gloves for the second time.

Jack Casey found employment with the building contractor, Lane Fox, working as a labourer on the building sites in Sunderland's East End. He was still recognised by many people in the streets of his home town, but he was no longer the celebrity he had been, in the early thirties. Sunderland had found other sporting heroes among the players of Sunderland AFC, who won the First Division championship in the 1935-36 season and the FA Cup, in 1937. Boxing itself was in eclipse in the town: the 'Royal' became a cinema, in 1936, and only minor bouts were staged at the Pottery Buildings and the Monkwearmouth Miners' Hall.

The Golden Lion Hotel in High Street East where Jack Casey had his gymnasium in the 1930s

44

Chapter 8

THE FELLOWSHIP OF THE RING

In 1939, Casey enlisted in the King's Own Scottish Borderers, and he performed a variety of duties during his time in the Army. He was a physical training instructor, guarded German prisoners in a POW camp, and served as a lance corporal in the Garrison Military Police. He had a few matches in Army boxing competitions, and, in 1942, he fought his last professional contest. On 22 February 1942, he faced a young Irish heavyweight, Martin Thornton, at Loughborough. Thornton, known as the 'Connemara Crusher', was being groomed for the Irish heavyweight championship. It had been four years since Casey had last fought professionally: he was ring-rusty, overweight and under-trained. The hard-hitting Thornton pounded Casey until the sixth round when, with Casey's face raw and bleeding, the referee stepped in to halt the contest. It was after this fight that Casey began to suffer headaches and black-outs, and he was re-mustered to the Pioneer Corps. He was posted to Cardiff, where he operated the smokescreens used to protect the docks during air-raids. In 1944, he was invalided out of the Army.

L.Cpl. Casey of the Garrison Military Police when stationed in Luton, 1941

Casey spent most of his invalidity leave indulging his passion for snooker in one of the halls in the town centre. He used to arrive early in the morning, change into slippers, and spend the whole day at the snooker tables, either playing or watching others make their strokes. He then worked for a time as a labourer on building sites, on the town's new housing estates. There followed another labouring job, this time in Greenwell's shipyard, on the Wear. His foreman used to complain that Casey could not get on with his work because he was always surrounded by other workers wanting him to talk about his fights. Another story is that Jack was once knocked down by a steel plate being swung into place by a crane and, as he lay on the ground, his workmates began to chant 'One...two...three..four', but Jack was soon up on his feet with the quip: 'I always beat the count.' In 1954, he took a job away from home, at the Grand Electric Combustion Company, in Derby. Both the general manager of the works and Casey's foreman at the plant had been boxing fans, in the 1930's, and they were happy to offer employment to the former fighter.

Elizabeth and Jack Casey at home in their terrace cottage.

However, Jack Casey's health began to deteriorate rapidly and he found he could no longer hold down a job. He began to put on weight, going up to 16stone 7lbs, and his face looked puffy and unhealthy. He developed chronic bronchitis and the doctors found that he suffered from anaemia. In the 1950's, he sold his semi-detached house near the seafront and moved to a terraced cottage, in the Roker area. Ownership of this modest cottage was all that he had to show for the twelve years he had spent in the ring. Not that Casey complained: 'I've no-one to blame but myself that I'm now down on luck and cash. I did make big money, but I spent

Bright Street where Jack Casey spent his retirement years.

Sunderland Ex-Boxers' Association.
left to right : Jack Casey, Tom Smith and Danny Veitch.

what I got.' His wife, Elizabeth, took a job in a tile factory to supplement his meagre sickness benefits. In the evenings, he played his accordion in public houses in return for a few drinks, and he still enjoyed a game of snooker.

These were bleak times for Jack Casey, broken in health and short of money, and his friends did what they could to help. The members of the Sunderland Ex-Boxers Association used to provide the funds to hire Jack a dinner jacket from Moss Brothers, to enable him to attend the annual dinner of the National Sporting Club in London. Here, Casey, as former Northern Area middleweight champion, mixed with other former champions and swapped yarns about the fight game; and, every year. he received a Christmas card from Len Harvey with a £5 note tucked inside it.

Jack Casey's health continued to decline. After piling on weight, he now began to lose it and had long spells in hospital. Then, in July 1973, the Sunderland Ex-Boxers Association organised a special social evening in his honour, at the Ford and Hylton Lane Social Club. The club was packed with former boxers and friends from all parts of the North East. The evening took the form of a 'This is your life' programme, and, among those present were eleven of Casey's former opponents: Gunner Ainsley, Dick Bartlett, Jim Britton, Andy Keating, Charlie McDonald, Andy McLaughlin, Fred Shaw, Johnny Summers, Danny Veitch, George Willis and Joe Woodie. Former members of Jack Casey's school of boxing turned out in force. Walker Russell, his old manager, was

*Jim Britton toasts the health of his former opponent, Jack Casey,
at the social evening held as a tribute to the old Assassin.*

there, as was Tom Crome, Vice President of the World Boxing Asociation. Tommy Farr, Len Harvey, Jack Hood and Fred Charlton sent letters of regard to the old Assassin. It was an evening of unrestrained nostalgia for those present, as old fights were recalled, and it culminated in the presentation of an album and wallet of notes to Jack Casey.

In 1976, Elizabeth Casey died. If Jack was a cast-iron man, then his wife was an iron lady. She had looked after her husband for over twenty years, as his health declined, and for seventeen years, she had combined this work with a full-time job in a tile factory. She had been helped by her two sons, John and George, who continued to support their father, after her death.

In 1978, the son of Archie Sexton, Dave, at that time the manager of Manchester United, travelled up to Sunderland to visit Jack Casey in hospital. Archie Sexton had retired from the ring in 1936 and, during the Second World War, he had served in the Special Constabulary. During the blitz on London, he had rescued several people buried under debris and was awarded the George Medal. After the war, he had emigrated to New Zealand where he died of a virus infection. Among his effects, he had left his son, Dave, a poster of the Casey-Sexton eliminating bout, staged at New St James' Hall, in 1932. The poster was one of Dave Sexton's most treasured possessions, as a souvenir of his father's boxing career. He always had a soft spot for his father's old opponent and, whenever his team played at Roker Park, he sought out the cast iron man for a chat.

Looking back on his ring career, in retirement, Casey picked out his fight with Marcel

Thil as the best performance of his career, and perhaps he was right in his choice. When Casey went to London to fight Thil, he was a little known provincial fighter matched against an opponent of world class, and he turned in a magnificent performance against the formidable Frenchman. Indeed, Thil regarded his fight with Casey as the hardest of his career, and when the Frenchman was interviewed by the journalist, Dixon Cairns, at Rheims, in 1945, he said: 'Your Jack Casey was the toughest and bravest man I ever fought.' Casey rated Len Harvey as the cleverest boxer he ever met, and his championship contest with Harvey must come a very close second to the Thil fight among Casey's best performances in the ring. Casey regarded Jock McAvoy as the hardest puncher he faced, and McAvoy, with his body punching, came closer than anyone else to putting Casey down on the canvas for the full count. Casey also remembered the German welterweight, Franz Kruppel, as being among the toughest opponents he had met in the ring.

The last years of Jack's life were a battle against poor health, and he died in hospital, on 24 January 1980. A service was held at Sunderland Parish Church and he was buried in Sunderland Cemetery. After his death, the Sunderland Ex-Boxers Association instituted the Jack Casey Trophy, in memory of the cast-iron man, which is awarded every year to the most promising amateur boxer in the Wearside area.

SUNDERLAND EX-BOXERS ASSOCIATION

Presents

A Social Evening

With a tribute to

JACK CASEY

SUNDERLAND

FORMER NORTHERN MIDDLEWEIGHT CHAMPION

ATTENDED BY A GALAXY OF STARS IN THE WORLD OF
SPORT AND ENTERTAINMENT

On Wednesday 11th July 1973
From 7-00 p.m. to 11-00 p.m.

At the Ford and Hylton Lane Social Club

ADMISSION 20p

JACK CASEY - AN ASSESSMENT

Casey is remembered by those who followed boxing during the inter-war years as a tough, colourful fighter, and some boxing buffs of the present day will be familiar with his record. Otherwise, he is largely a forgotten figure. As a boxer, Jack Casey fought the best in the game. He was Northern Area middleweight champion 1932-34, but he never won a British title. He beat Jock McAvoy and Archie Sexton in eliminating bouts and he came close to defeating Len Harvey in their British middleweight championship fight, but he could not clinch victory and therefore his name never entered the record books as title holder. Casey might have fought for the British light heavyweight championship when he moved up into the cruiserweight class, but he mismanaged his career and muffed his chances of securing a second title fight. It must be concluded that he was among the best of the middleweights and cruiserweights of his time but he was not good enough to win a British title. Similarly, he did well in the opening rounds of his fight with Marcel Thil, then allowed Thil to recover and go on to win the fight. A victory over the great French fighter would have been something to be remembered for but Casey could not quite manage it.

Jack Casey's claim to fame, perhaps, rests upon another aspect of his ring career, as the 'cast iron' man of British boxing. In over 200 fights, he was never counted out, and he faced some of the hardest punchers of his time, including men far heavier than himself. Marcel Thil, who was no milksop, described Casey as 'the toughest man in the world', and Jim Kenrick, who refereed the Casey-Seelig fight, afterwards observed:

> *'While refereeing the fight between Casey and Seelig, my thoughts went to Battling Nelson. Casey is just such another; he seems to thrive on punishment and punches bounce off him as if his jaw were made of india-rubber. You can take my word for it, the German is no snowflake puncher. Every punch he sends out has all the weight of his body behind it, and every punch is correct. There is no wild slugging, no hitting with the inside of the glove or any slapping. Short, stabbing punches which jar and hurt, in short punches packed with dynamite. Yet Casey collected these in a most matter-of-fact manner.'*

Casey has often been compared to Battling Nelson, the 'durable Dane'. Nelson's boxing career in American rings spanned the years 1896-1917, and he held the world lightweight championship 1908-10. He was knocked out twice in 131 fights. Some boxing pundits would put forward the claims of Joe Grim, an Italian-American fighter known as the 'Iron Man', who is said to have taken part in several hundred contests.

Was Casey, then, the toughest of them all? The question is sometimes discussed among boxing buffs and, in my view, it is impossible to answer. Comparisons between fighters, especially when they fought in different periods and in different rings, are very dubious. Certainly, we are on much safer ground in saying that Casey's inter-war record entitles him to be bracketed with Battling Nelson and Joe Grim, the 'iron men' of an earlier period of boxing, and that, perhaps, Casey's name should join theirs in the various encyclopediae of boxing. It is certain that there could never be another Casey in boxing because present day boxers are not allowed to fight as often as Casey did, medical inspections are more strict, and modern referees step in earlier to save boxers from taking excessive punishment. The days of 'iron men' soaking up punches and battling it out against the odds until the final bell are now over.

What made Casey so tough? This is another question often asked. Both Len Harvey and Jack London injured their right hands on his jaw and two of Casey's sparring partners fractured bones in their hands, during training sessions. All sorts of reasons were advanced to explain his imperviousness to a knock-out blow. It was said that his spinal cord was not connected to his brain, that the nerve on the point of the chin which connects to the brain was missing, or that he had a double jaw bone. Medical tests showed that none of the theories was true. An examination of his jaw, including an X-ray, carried out, in 1969, did reveal that Casey had good quality bone, his masseteric muscles (used for chewing) were well developed, as was the mandibular conduyles which links the jaw with the skull, and this, according to the examining doctor 'could have served as a cushion against hard blows'. Casey's explanation for this state was that his love of sea food - whelks, crabs and prawns - which he had consumed in vast quantities since he was a small boy, had developed his jaw muscles and provided the phosphorus and calcium which had strengthened the bone in his jaw. Whatever the reason, Casey was blessed with a 'cast iron' jaw which made him the toughest fighter of the inter-war period, certainly on this side of the Atlantic.

Yet Casey was something more than a human punch-bag and, in putting the emphasis on Casey's toughness, we should not overlook another aspect of his fighting qualities: his punching power, which gained him the cognomen, the 'Sunderland Assassin'.
Casey could deliver a knock-out punch with either hand. Both his left hook and his right cross were capable of putting a man on the canvas and, because he had little need to worry about defence, he could throw punches from all angles. He was immensely strong and would wear down an opponent with constant pressure until he judged the time was ripe to move in for the 'kill'. As Len Harvey recalled:

> 'If ever a man looked every inch a fighter, it was Jack Casey
> as he came crouching over his gloves to meet me. His bullet
> head, his broken nose, his big square-jawed face - all these
> loudly advertised his profession; but more impressive still
> were his great shoulders, bulging with muscle and tapering
> into the slim waist of a true athlete.'

One final attribute of Casey's was his boxing skill. This may surprise some people who think of Casey as a tough, hard punching but essentially crude fighter. Certainly, Casey was no exponent of the classical style of boxing. Someone once said that fighting Casey was like being in the ring with a concrete-mixer. If Casey thought he could take a man early in a fight, he would bore in and finish him off. Otherwise he would wear his opponent down before moving in to strike the final blow. However, he acquired considerable ring experience over the years and he could box with skill to get the result he wanted. Casey used these tactics to good effect in his fights with Len Harvey and Tommy Farr. He narrowly failed to beat Harvey but he did defeat Farr. Casey knew that both men were boxers of outstanding ability and to rush in throwing punches at them would be to invite defeat. It is also sometimes overlooked that Casey had a powerful left jab, and it was this punch which did the damage to Archie Sexton in their eliminating contest for the middleweight championship.

Toughness, punching power, strength and skill, Casey had them all, and he also had something else which endeared him to the fans: he had personality. In and out of the ring, he was a 'character', and it was sad to witness his decline after he had retired from the ring. He never lost the affection of his fellow professionals and the boxing fans who had followed his career, and in the last years of his life, he received, in some measure, the recognition which was his due.

JACK CASEY'S FIGHTING RECORD 1926-1942

Fight		Opponent	Result	by	Round	Venue
1	17 Jul 1926	W. Teasdale	won	K.O.	1	Sunderland
2	17 Jul 1926	J. Britton	drew		4	Sunderland
3	6 Nov 1926	J. Britton	lost	Points	6	Sunderland
4	20 Dec 1926	George Willis	drew		6	North Shields
5	8 Jan 1927	George Willis	won	Points	6	Jarrow
6	17 Jan 1927	Young Scott	won	Points	6	Hetton-on-Hole
7	29 Jan 1927	Teddy Welsh	lost	Points	6	South Shields
8	7 Feb 1927	Alf Bainbridge	lost	Points	6	North Shields
9	19 Mar 1927	Eddie McGurk	drew		6	Tyne Dock
10	28 Mar 1927	Eddie McGurk	lost	Points	6	Tyne Dock
11	2 Apr 1927	Alf Smith	won	Retired	4	North Shields
12	16 Apr 1927	Joe Kennedy	won	Points	6	Tyne Dock
13	30 Apr 1927	Eddie McGurk	won	Points	6	Sunderland
14	16 May 1927	Teddy Welsh	won	Points	6	Newcastle
15	21 May 1927	Owen McIvor	won	Retired	4	Sunderland
16	4 Jun 1927	Jim Britton	won	Points	6	Washington
17	11 Jun 1927	Jim Britton	drew		6	Sunderland
18	18 Jun 1927	Barney Ward	won	K.O.	3	Tyne Dock
19	2 Jul 1927	Slogger Bingham	won	Points	6	Tyne Dock
20	6 Aug 1927	Jack Graham	won	Points	10	Tyne Dock
21	29 Aug 1927	Phil Guerin	won	Retired	3	Newcastle
22	10 Sep 1927	Owen McIvor	won	K.O.	2	Sunderland
23	17 Sep 1927	Tommy East	won	Referee stopped fight	5	Newcastle
24	24 Sep 1927	Danny Veitch	won	Points	10	Sunderland
25	1 Oct 1927	Young Josephs	won	Referee stopped fight	7	Newcastle
26	8 Oct 1927	Joe Woodie	won	Points	6	Sunderland
27	10 Oct 1927	Joe Kennedy	won	Referee stopped fight	6	Tyne Dock
28	24 Oct 1927	Pat Crawford	won	Retired	8	Newcastle
29	4 Nov 1927	Peel Bell	lost	Retired	8	Carlisle
30	12 Nov 1927	Bob Phillips	won	Points	10	Sunderland
31	3 Dec 1927	Bob Phillips	won	Points	10	Newcastle
32	12 Dec 1927	Pat Crawford	lost	Retired	4	Newcastle
33	17 Dec 1927	Dave Dowd	won	Points	10	Sunderland
34	26 Dec 1927	Jim Birch	lost	Points	10	Leeds
35	14 Jan 1928	Con Tansey	won	Retired	7	Sunderland
36	21 Jan 1928	Young Griffo	won	Referee stopped fight	7	Sunderland
37	30 Jan 1928	Pat Crawford	won	Disqualification	5	Newcastle
38	20 Feb 1928	Tommy Woods	drew		10	Tyne Dock
39	4 Mar 1928	Billy Mack	won	Points	10	Leeds
40	10 Mar 1928	Jack Turner	lost	Points	10	Sunderland
41	17 Mar 1928	Andy Keating	won	Points	10	Tyne Dock
42	14 Apr 1928	Joe Grewer	won	Points	10	Sunderland
43	2 Jun 1928	Terry Donlon	won	Retired	7	Aston under Lyne
44	16 Jun 1928	Stan Bradbury	won	Points	10	Aston under Lyne
45	8 Jul 1928	Al Kenny	drew		15	Salford
46	20 Jul 1928	Charlie Dickenson	lost	Points	15	Openshaw
47	7 Aug 1928	Jim Harrison	won	K.O.	3	Aston under Lyne
48	19 Aug 1928	Jock McFarlane	won	Points	15	Royton
49	24 Aug 1928	Jack Hines	lost	Points	15	Openshaw

53

Fight		Opponent		Result by	Round	Venue
50	1 Sep 1928	Joe Grewer	won	Retired	7	Sunderland
51	29 Sep 1928	Charlie Dickenson	won	Retired	7	Sunderland
52	5 Oct 1928	Young Giffo	lost	Points	15	Newcastle
53	27 Oct 1928	Paul McGuire	won	Points	12	Sunderland
54	4 Nov 1928	Lion Smith	won	Referee stopped fight	1	Leeds
55	13 Nov 1928	Peter Bottomley	won	Points	10	Edinburgh
56	18 Nov 1928	Ernest Kaye	won	Points	12	Leeds
57	23 Nov 1928	Charlie Lee	won	Referee stopped fight	3	Darlington
58	1 Dec 1928	Ted Abbott	won	Points	15	Sunderland
59	7 Dec 1928	Alec Law	won	Disqualification	6	Darlington
60	9 Dec 1928	Dino Guselli	won	Points	15	Royton
61	16 Dec 1928	Ernest Kaye	won	Points	12	Leeds
62	21 Dec 1928	Ernest Kaye	drew		12	Hartlepool
63	12 Jan 1929	Jack Harbin	lost	Points	12	Sunderland
64	21 Jan 1929	Willie Upton	lost	Points	12	Edinburgh
65	27 Jan 1929	Fred Oldfield	won	Points	12	Leeds
66	8 Feb 1929	Ted Abbott	drew		15	Darlington
67	16 Feb 1929	Peter Kelly	won	Points	12	Sunderland
68	22 Feb 1929	Ted Abbott	drew		12	Darlington
69	24 Feb 1929	Tom Gregson	won	Referee stopped fight	8	Leeds
70	2 Mar 1929	Jack Harbin	lost	Points	12	Newcastle
71	11 Mar 1929	Bob Cockburn	won	Points	12	Edinburgh
72	18 Mar 1929	Ted Abbott	won	Points	15	South Shields
73	23 Mar 1929	Franz Kruppel	lost	Points	15	Sunderland
74	20 Apr 1929	Jack Marshall	won	Points	15	Sunderland
75	28 Apr 1929	Seaman Smart	won	Retired	6	Leeds
76	19 May 1929	Pat O'Brien	lost	Points	15	Leeds
77	25 May 1929	Franz Kruppel	won	Points	15	Sunderland
78	6 Jun 1929	Albert Johnson	lost	Retired	7	Sunderland
79	16 Jun 1929	Albert Johnson	lost	Points	12	Leeds
80	29 Jun 1929	Fred Oldfield	lost	Points	15	Sunderland
81	2 Aug 1929	Albert Johnson	lost	Points	15	Middlesbrough
82	24 Aug 1929	George Willis	lost	Points	15	Sunderland
83	25 Aug 1929	Alec Thake	won	Points	15	Leeds
84	21 Sep 1929	George Willis	lost	Points	15	Sunderland
85	4 Oct 1929	Ted Robinson	drew		12	Preston
86	19 Oct 1929	Albert Johnson	lost	Referee stopped fight	6	Sunderland
87	25 Oct 1929	Ted Robinson	won	Points	12	Preston
88	2 Nov 1929	Mick Harris	won	K.O.	6	Sunderland
89	9 Nov 1929	Fred Oldfield	drew		15	Hartlepool
90	9 Dec 1929	Joe Woodruff	lost	Points	15	Hartlepool
91	27 Dec 1929	Jim Pearson	won	Retired	8	Preston
92	30 Dec 1929	Fred Oldfield	won	Points	15	Hartlepool
93	3 Jan 1930	Joe Lowther	lost	Points	15	Hull
94	13 Jan 1930	Joe Lowther	lost	Points	15	Hull
95	25 Jan 1930	Jerry Daley	won	Retired	6	Sunderland
96	9 Feb 1930	Dick Burt	won	Points	12	Leeds
97	16 Feb 1930	Hal O'Neill	won	Points	12	Leeds
98	22 Feb 1930	Sonny Bird	won	Points	15	Sunderland
99	16 Mar 1930	Hal O'Neill	won	Retired	8	Leeds
100	24 Mar 1930	Wattie Wilde	won	Referee stopped fight	5	West Hartlepool

Fight		Opponent	Result by		Round	Venue
101	29 Mar 1930	Archie Sexton	lost	Points	15	Sunderland
102	4 Apl 1930	George Porter	won	Points	12	Bradford
103	11 Apr 1930	Jack Haynes	drew		15	Barnsley
104	19 Apr 1930	Farmer Jackson	won	Retired	11	Sunderland
105	28 Apr 1930	Sandy McKenzie	lost	Points	15	West Hartlepool
106	3 May 1930	Jack Haynes	won	Disqualification	6	Sunderland
107	12 May 1930	Sandy McKenzie	lost	Points	15	Newcastle
108	31 May 1930	Charlie McDonald	lost	Points	15	Sunderland
109	13 Jun 1930	Joe Woodruff	won	Points	12	Preston
110	21 Jun 1930	Bert Mottram	won	Disqualification	4	Crook
111	28 Jun 1930	Pat Casey	won	Retired	7	Newcastle
112	11 Jul 1930	Roy Martin	won	Referee stopped fight	3	Preston
113	20 Jul 1930	Fred Oldfield	won	Retired	5	Leeds
114	25 Jul 1930	Hal O'Neill	won	Retired	7	Preston
115	17 Aug 1930	Joe Lowther	won	Points	12	Leeds
116	20 Aug 1930	Gunner Ainsley	won	Retired	3	West Hartlepool
117	30 Aug 1930	Ted Coveney	won	Retired	5	Newcastle
118	10 Sep 1930	Joe Woodruff	won	Points	12	Harrogate
119	17 Sep 1930	Joe Woodruff	won	Points	15	Morecombe
120	20 Sep 1930	Billy Roberts	won	Retired	4	Newcastle
121	30 Sep 1930	Jerry Daley	won	Retired	6	Manchester
122	5 Oct 1930	Fred Shaw	won	Points	12	Leeds
123	10 Oct 1930	Joe Lowther	lost	Retired	11	Preston
124	9 Nov 1930	Harry Mason	lost	Points	12	Leeds
125	17 Nov 1930	Sandy McKenzie	lost	Points	15	Glasgow
126	9 Dec 1930	Sandy McKenzie	won	Referee stopped fight	7	Manchester
127	21 Dec 1930	Joe Lowther	won	Points	12	Leeds
128	1 Jan 1931	Joe Woodruff	won	Points	12	Barnsley
129	3 Jan 1931	Archie Sexton	won	Retired	9	Manchester
130	18 Jan 1931	Fred Shaw	lost	Points	12	Leeds
131	27 Jan 1931	Jack Hood	lost	Points	15	Manchester
132	16 Feb 1931	Phil Green	lost	Points	10	Newcastle
133	23 Feb 1931	Fred Shaw	lost	Points	12	Leeds
134	2 Mar 1931	Jack O'Brien	won	Points	10	Leeds
135	9 Mar 1931	George Willis	won	Retired	10	Newcastle
136	17 Mar 1931	Jack O'Brien	won	Retired	7	Manchester
137	22 Mar 1931	Jack O'Brien	won	K.O.	3	Leeds
138	10 Apr 1931	Jack Haynes	won	K.O.	2	Preston
139	4 May 1931	George Gordon	won	K.O.	2	Newcastle
140	6 Jun 1931	Fred Shaw	won	Retired	12	Barnsley
141	12 Jun 1931	Jack Haynes	won	K.O.	1	Middlesbrough
143	29 Jun 1931	Dick Bartlett	won	K.O.	2	Hartlepool
144	27 Jul 1931	Sonny Doke	drew		15	West Hartlepool
144	3 Jul 1931	Fred Shaw	won	Retired	4	Preston
145	3 Aug 1931	Archie Sexton	drew		15	South Shields
146	5 Aug 1931	Dixie Cullen	won	Retired	5	Hartlepool
147	11 Sep 1931	Glen Moody	won	Referee stopped fight	4	Manchester
148	10 Sep 1931	Fred Shaw	won	Points	12	Leeds
149	19 Oct 1931	Joe Rostrom	won	Referee stopped fight	7	West Hartlepool
150	9 Nov 1931	Marcel Thil	lost	Points	10	London
151	16 Nov 1931	Joe Woodruff	won	Referee stopped fight	3	Manchester
152	23 Nov 1931	Bob McGuffog	won	Referee stopped fight	3	Newcastle

Fight		Opponent	Result by		Round	Venue
153	7 Dec 1931	Harry Mason	won	Disqualification	3	Leeds
154	16 Dec 1931	Seaman Harvey	lost	Points	6	London
155	28 Dec 1931	Billy Adair	won	Retired	3	Newcastle
156	18 Jan 1932	Dick Bartlett	won	K.O.	2	Manchester
157	8 Feb 1932	Len Harvey	lost	Points	15	Newcastle
158	14 Mar 1932	Seaman Harvey	won	Retired	3	Newcastle
159	1 Apr 1932	Sandy McKenzie	won	K.O.	2	Middlesbrough
160	8 Apr 1932	Jack Marshall	won	Referee stopped fight	6	Blackburn
161	22 Apr 1932	Hal O'Neill	won	Referee stopped fight	2	Middlesbrough
162	6 May 1932	Red Pullen	won	K.O.	5	West Hartlepool
163	27 May 1932	Les Saunders	won	K.O.	4	Nelson
164	30 May 1932	Glen Moody	won	Points	12	Birmingham
165	9 Jun 1932	Eddie Strawer	won	Points	12	Douglas (I of M)
166	19 Jun 1932	Billy Thomas	won	Referee stopped fight	3	Royton
167	18 Jul 1932	Jock McAvoy	won	Disqualification	14	Manchester
168	1 Aug 1932	George Porter	won	K.O.	2	Sunderland
169	4 Aug 1932	Glen Moody	won	K.O.	2	West Hartlepool
170	3 Oct 1932	Archie Sexton	won	K.O.	7	Newcastle
171	16 Oct 1932	George Brown	won	Points	10	Leeds
172	31 Oct 1932	Del Fontaine	won	K.O.	4	Newcastle
173	14 Nov 1932	Glen Moody	won	Referee stopped fight	3	Newcastle
174	12 Dec 1932	Len Harvey	lost	Points	15	Newcastle
175	9 Jan 1933	Eddie Maguire	won	Points	12	Newcastle
176	27 Jan 1933	Seaman Harvey	won	Points	15	Plymouth
177	6 Feb 1933	Leo Bandias	won	Retired	12	Newcastle
178	27 Feb 1933	Eddie Maguire	won	K.O.	3	Newcastle
179	9 Mar 1933	Eddie Robinson	won	Referee stopped fight	4	Liverpool
180	13 Mar 1933	Eddie Maguire	lost	Points	12	Newcastle
181	10 Apr 1933	Archie Sexton	lost	Points	12	Manchester
182	22 Apr 1933	Joe Woodruff	won	Retired	6	Carlisle
183	7 May 1933	Les Ward	won	Retired	5	Royton
184	24 May 1933	Carmelo Candel	lost	Retired	5	Paris
185	6 Jun 1933	Dino Guselli	won	Retired	2	Inverness
186	12 Jun 1933	Jack London	won	Retired	10	West Hartlepool
187	26 Jun 1933	Ernie Simmons	lost	Points	10	Leicester
188	25 Aug 1933	Billy Wallace	won	Referee stopped fight	3	Darlington
189	3 Sep 1933	Reg Perkins	lost	Points	12	Middlesbrough
190	11 Sep 1933	Ernie Simmons	lost	Points	12	West Hartlepool
191	7 Oct 1933	Johnny Summers	won	Retired	12	Sunderland
192	23 Oct 1933	Paul Schaefer	won	Points	12	Manchester
193	3 Nov 1933	Andy McLaughlin	won	Points	12	North Shields
194	11 Dec 1933	Eddie Maguire	drew		15	Hull
195	22 Jan 1934	Johnny Summers	won	Points	12	York
196	3 Feb 1934	Les Ward	won	Retired	3	Sunderland
197	19 Feb 1934	Bushman Dempster	won	Retired	6	Edinburgh
198	13 Mar 1934	Jack Marshall	won	Retired	6	Aston under Lyme
199	19 Mar 1934	Reggie Meen	won	Disqualification	7	Newcastle
200	2 Apr 1934	Dave Sullivan	won	Retired	2	Aston under Lyme
201	9 Apr 1934	Charlie Belanger	won	Disqualification	7	Newcastle
202	23 Apr 1934	Tommy Farr	won	Points	12	Newcastle
203	21 May 1934	George Slack	won	Points	10	Newcastle

Fight		Opponent	Result	by	Round	Venue
204	25 Jul 1934	Erich Seelig	lost	Points	12	Wandsworth
205	27 Aug 1934	Paul Schaefer	lost	Points	12	Newcastle
206	10 Sep 1934	Manuel Abrew	lost	Points	10	Newcastle
207	9 Oct 1934	Jack Sharkey	won	Retired	3	Hanley
208	15 Oct 1934	Bushman Dempster	won	Points	12	Carlisle
209	29 Oct 1934	Phil Munro	won	K.O.	7	Newcastle
210	12 Nov 1934	Bushman Dempster	won	Disqualification	11	West Hartlepool
211	17 Nov 1934	Ginger Hauxwell	won	K.O.	7	Sunderland
212	5 Dec 1934	Leonard Steyaert	lost	Points	12	York
213	17 Dec 1934	Jimmy Tarante	lost	Points	12	Newcastle
214	21 Jan 1935	Charlie Smith	lost	Retired	7	Newcastle
215	8 Apr 1935	Helmuth Hartkopp	lost	Points	12	Newcastle
216	28 May 1935	Jack London	lost	Points	12	Sunderland
217	6 Dec 1937	Jack Moran	lost	Points	10	Newcastle
218	20 Dec 1937	Reggie Meen	won	Referee stopped fight	2	Newcastle
219	17 Jan 1938	Ron Lindley	won	Points	5	Bradford
220	31Jan 1938	Stan Kirby	lost	Points	10	Darlington
221	21 Feb 1938	Jim McKenzie	lost	Points	10	Newcastle
222	21 Mar 1938	Zachy Nicholas	lost	Points	10	Penzance
223	31 Mar 1938	Packy Paul	lost	Retired	3	Sheffield
224	22 Feb 1942	Martin Thornton	lost	Referee stopped fight	6	Loughborough

Total Bouts : 224

Won	148	- 57 on points; 39 opponent retired; 22 referee stopped fight 21 by knock-out; 9 with disqualification.
Lost	61	- 52 on points; 8 retired and 1 referee stopped fight.
Drawn	15	

Although Casey was never knocked out eight men stopped him inside the distance :

> Peel Bell [1927]
> Pat Crawford [1927]
> Albert Johnson [twice in 1929]
> Joe Lowther [1930]
> Carmelo Candel [1933]
> Charlie Smith [1935]
> Packy Paul [1938]
> Martin Thornton [1942]

BIBLIOGRAPHY

Corfe, T.A.A   *History of Sunderland* (1973)

Hugman, Barry J.   *British Boxing Yearbooks* (1985-91)

Mason, Tony (ed.)   *Sport in Britain - a social history* (1984).
                                Ch.3 'Boxing' by Stan Shipley.

McGhee, Frank   *England's Boxing Heroes* (1988)

Milburn G.E.
and Miller, S.T. (Eds.)   *Sunderland: River, Town and People* (1988)

Moffatt, F.C.   *Linament and Leather: Sixty years of
                                the fight game in the North* (1982).

Odd, Gilbert   *Len Harvey: Prince of Boxers* (1978)

Odd, Gilbert   *The Encyclopedia of Boxing* (1989 ed)

Summerskill, Edith   *The Ignoble Art* (1956)

Wilson, Peter   *Ringside Seat* (1949)

Files of :
Birmingham Mail, Boxing, Boxing News, Daily Express, Daily Mirror, Empire News, London Evening News, Manchester Evening News, Newcastle Evening Chronicle, Newcastle Journal, Northern Daily Mail, Northern Echo, Sunderland Echo, Sunday People, Sunday Sun, Topical Times, Weekly Chronicle and Yorkshire Evening Press, with special reference to Fred Charlton's articles in 'Round the Rings' which appeared in the *Sunderland Echo* 1955-71.